KNOW
THE
MYSTERY

KNOW
THE
MYSTERY

That if that which you seek you find
not within yourself, you will
never find it without

Mary Scott Daugherty

SUNSTONE
PRESS

SANTA FE

Sunstone books may be purchased for educational, business, or sales promotional use.
For information please write: Special Markets Department, Sunstone Press,
P.O. Box 2321, Santa Fe, New Mexico 87504-2321.

Book design I Vicki Ahl
body typeface I Arial ▲ Display typeface I Colonna MT
Printed on acid free paper

Library of Congress Cataloging-in-Publication Data

Daugherty, Mary Scott, 1934-
  Know the mystery : for if that which you seek you find not within yourself, you will never
find it without / by Mary Scott Daugherty.
      p. cm.
  Includes bibliographical references.
  ISBN 978-0-86534-598-0 (softcover : alk. paper)
  1. Daugherty, Mary Scott, 1934- 2. Feminists--Biography. I. Title.
  HQ1413.D26A3 2008
  305.42092--dc22
  [B]
                                          2008018003

Published in

WWW.SUNSTONEPRESS.COM
SUNSTONE PRESS / POST OFFICE BOX 2321 / SANTA FE, NM 87504-2321 /USA
(505) 988-4418 / ORDERS ONLY (800) 243-5644 / FAX (505) 988-1025

Lovingly dedicated
to
My Grandmother
My Mother
My Children
and
Myself

CONTENTS

PREFACE

I call these personal essays "radical feminist Self help." I capitalize Self because when I first read it that way in Mary Daly's writing, I knew that within *me* was something real and important and what I had been seeking. There was "somebody *in* there" and I wanted her to come forth. I came to refer to her as my True Self, or my Essential Self, or my Original Self. So you see, a majorly important concept gets capitalized. It's a big deal. As for the pieces being helpful, they contain parts of my life from which I have learned. Perhaps they will be useful for you.

They started when I highlighted portions of my journals of 1983-1993. I highlighted in different colors and noticed that I had about nine different subjects. I copied everything that was in each color and that became the beginning of a personal essay. Over the fourteen years of working with these essays I have added to and changed them.

Essentially, these essays are about Self awareness. Certainly, they are about Growing and Changing. I was desperate to know and Be with my Self. And, gratefully, this happened. I found that my Self was like a good parent—patient and nurturing. She showed me what I wanted and needed to know—naming it and guiding me to know how to do it.

So I found that the Real-ization of all that I sought came from within me. Thus, the title of this book.

I AM A WOMAN
GIVING BIRTH
TO MYSELF ·

The birth chant from Ellen's story, from It's All Right to be Woman Theatre.

The birth chant from Ellen's story from It's All Right to be Woman Theatre, courtesy of Times Change Press.

BE—COMING

For some of us, there comes a time in our lives when we must change or die—literally or metaphorically. It can be unforgettably intense, unsettling, and difficult for us and for the people in our lives, yet it feels completely right. For me, it was the break I had been waiting for all of my conscious life. I was forty-one years old when it came. I had been married twenty years and was the mother of three children. For years I had been writing in a journal, contemplating suicide daily, and reading every piece of feminist writing I could find. I did post graduate work, radical political work, and I helped organize the first two women's consciousness raising groups in San Antonio, Texas. I taught for a year in an alternative school. I was in therapy throughout this time, but no matter what I did, I couldn't, as the Shaker hymn says: "come down where I ought to be." It got worse and worse.

One day I snapped and swallowed every sleeping pill I could find in the medicine cabinet. It was a desperate move, but what was really important about it eluded me until just recently, more than twenty-five years later. What I realized was that in attempting to end my life I had also been given the chance to save my life. After hearing a voice that told me I was a "good girl" for keeping the pills down, I defied it and had myself taken to an emergency room to have my stomach pumped out. That decision—saving my life—seemed to put me in the readiness position I needed in order to make the next right moves. It was like a sardonic miracle, for suddenly everything began to fall into place and I began to know what to do with myself. A few weeks after my suicide attempt I came home from my teaching job, sat down on my bed, and *knew* that I was going to leave my family. I also had the strong feeling that I would go to Boston. I think Boston represented freedom (The Freedom Trail, the Boston Tea Party), resistance (protests for ending the war in Vietnam) and learning (all the universities and colleges in the area). Also, Thoreau's Walden Pond was nearby.

None of this was alarming, but I did wonder what I would do in Boston. The answer came quickly: I would go to school. I pulled down a copy of the *New Woman's Survival Catalogue* from a shelf above my bed, looked in the education section and saw that in Boston there was a school called Goddard Cambridge Graduate School for Social Change. I liked the sound of it, sent them a request for a catalogue and in two months was in Boston checking it out. My breakthrough was just like that—sudden, fast and productive.

Of course, the reality of actually leaving San Antonio was so difficult that I dissociated from it. I took care of business, but I was unable to be emotionally aware of myself or intelligible to others about what I was doing. I was pretty much in a haze, which was probably what protected me from totally caving in and giving up. The miracle was that I never lost the sense of the rightness of my going to Boston or of my determination to do it. Leaving my daughter was unbelievably hard, and it still breaks my heart to remember the look of confusion on my youngest son's face the day I left. But, in spite of these incredibly painful moments and in spite of the fact that I made the move without anyone understanding what I was doing or supporting me emotionally, I would do it again. Actually, I don't believe that I *could* have done anything else.

When I got to Boston, one of my teachers said to me: "You seem to have a sense of destiny." I had no idea what she meant. Now I know that she realized I was on a mission, but at that time I was too afraid to acknowledge that what I had done was either right or good, much less purposeful. How could I? I was doing something outrageous which made no sense to anyone that I knew. As a revered woman in San Antonio said to me just before I was about to leave for Boston: "You have a wonderful husband and three outstanding children. You're rich and you're beautiful. There must me something wrong with you." I knew there wasn't *anything* wrong with me, but I didn't yet have the words to intelligibly defend myself—or the courage.

After thirty years, that is no longer the case. I can now articulate, to my satisfaction, what going to Boston was all about and I can also talk about what has worked since then to help me keep changing and be-coming ever new.

On the wall of my apartment in Somerville, Massachusetts, was a poster that read: "I am a woman giving birth to myself." That's what Boston was all about. It was as simple and as complicated as that. Now the poster hangs above my desk. I still love what it says and I love that what it says is still true of me.

As for what works to keep me giving birth to myself, there are two things that are indispensable: solitude and journaling.

Before I went to Boston, I was radically removed from myself. I not only didn't know *who* I was; I didn't know *that* I was. I felt that I had to separate from the world that I knew in order to know that I even *existed*—that I was real. I had to get away from what Mary Daly calls "the noise of the fore-ground." I lived alone for my first year in Boston and rarely felt lonely because I was busy and I was intrigued with everything I was able to do and see. Just about anything could make my day. Then, during my second year, I lived in a house with three other women where we each had our own bedroom. In that household, amidst others, I got used to being able to shut my door and feel not only safe behind it, but productive as well. I found out that I could lead a very rich life all by myself— even when there were others around.

I also learned a lot about me when I was with others. I had been an only and neglected child and never really had a friend but I learned early on that if I was outgoing and attentive to others, I could survive socially. That skill worked well for me in Boston, but I began to have experiences with others that suggested that maybe I wasn't the "people person" that I, and everyone else, thought I was. I realized that I usually felt quite lonely when I was with others and very out of the loop. When I began to process all this, I found that being alone in my room helped. No one was there to intervene and I could get hold of what was going on. I made a tiny beginning and wrote my graduating paper from Goddard Cambridge on "The Concept and Experience of Separateness."

When I returned to San Antonio after two and a half years, I divorced and lived alone. For three years I was very active in the women's community and rapturously in love with the women in my life. Then I began to have the same out-of-the-loop feelings I had had in Boston. As I told one woman: "I'm a feminist and I'm afraid of the girls." So I withdrew and entered a time of isolation, deep introspection and a study of radical feminist thought. This time, being alone was different and harder. Blessedly, I was neither agitated nor restless; I was content to just sit and be with myself.

My cat and a stone I held were the only witnesses to what was going on. At first I could feel only Absence, but gradually I began to feel and face my emptiness and the anxiety that went along with it. I went as deep as I could and I *thought* about how I felt. Because I was alone, no one could interfere with my process.

During those years, I went into the hidden and repressed realities of my past. At first I was like that stunned and stopped deer caught in the lights of an oncoming car. Most of the time I felt weak and insecure and I was glad there was no one around who might be frightened by these very natural feelings. I also needed to be alone in order to discover and focus on an alternative to the trance that enticed me. By trance, I mean a total shut down. I would get so scared that I would space out in order not to feel. I wouldn't run; I would just freeze. Since I was alone, I could bear with myself. Then, if I was willing to stay with a scary feeling long enough and it became more familiar, I was less afraid of it. I managed to talk myself through it—gently and like a loving parent—until I could see it without needing to run from it. I faced, and began to make a blessed peace with, the neglect and abuses of my childhood—ones that had held me terrorized and frozen in repetitive behavior that I hoped would get me the love and attention I'd never known. As I am now on the other side of this "facing", I know that this was essential work, for if I had not done it, I would have been doomed to stay caught up in the "fixtures" of my family history—what was *familiar*. For me to heal and change the behaviors I learned in the cauldron of my family, I had to separate from those who affected me.

As I write this, it's been thirty years since I went to Boston to begin finding and changing my life and I am more committed than ever to solitude. Sometimes I want to run from it. I fantasize a lover or go way outside my boundaries in order to *make* a friend, but again and again and again, I realize that solitude is essential for me to grow and change—to keep on be-coming—to keep on giving birth to myself.

The other thing that is essential to me is journaling. I was about thirty-three when I started journaling. At first I was just trying to say how I felt as best as I could. I was pitifully inarticulate, but for the first time in my life I was saying how I felt. Mostly what came out was how unhappy I was—and how afraid. As I kept journaling, I still told myself how I was feeling but I began to write words that answered and helped. One day I was very depressed and lost and contemplating going to a therapist. In my journal, I kept telling it like it was and asking for help. Before long I wrote: "What comes forth from me is my self help." I go to my journal whenever I am lost, which is nearly everyday when I wake. By the time I lay it down, I am usually found. The more I write, the more I want me and the more I need to hear from me. This is an amazing proof of Knowing the Mystery. That is: What I had been longing for all my life—to be wanted and for *them* to want to hear from me—I find within the conversation with myself.

I also have a little book in which I write three line poems— five syllables or less in the first line, seven or less in the second and five or less in the third. Sometimes, as I am writing in my journal, something *pithy* comes to me and I record it in my little blue book. I refer to these poems often and receive great help from them, for they are the essence of what I know and have learned. They are articulate clarity.

In addition to solitude and journaling, there are some other things that have helped and seem almost essential, too.

A very important one is that I'm not inclined to hang on to blaming others for the discomfort I feel. That does not mean that I don't realize the part they've played or in some cases, hold them accountable. It just means that once I've done that, I get on with what is more important to me. If I am obsessed with resentment I feel impotent and anxious. If I give the situation enough time and thought, however, I get back to myself and the priority of myself. I let *them* go—realize our separateness—and get on with my growth and change.

Another thing is to know that the process of self be-coming is different for each of us because each one of us is deconstructing a different set of hand-me-downs. Each of us has a unique self—our original self—to be-come, so it is important not to compare. As a therapist said to me once, "At the end of your life, Scottie, you won't be asked how much like someone else you became, but how much like your self you became." The more I know myself—be myself—the easier it is not to compare. I am enough.

Also, I have had to be so committed to my change that I am unable to fake satisfaction. I have made lots of mistakes along the way, but I know (by the way I know) when I am not getting it right—when I am not real-ly satisfied with what's going on. Then it is that I stop and withdraw and think about what has happened. These are times when I fill many, many pages in my journal.

Another critical aspect of my self be-coming is that, in the beginning, as I entered the process, I kept going whether I was misunderstood, disapproved of or shunned. It was as if I had no vulnerability. This is so very strange, yet blessed, since I was going through seemingly unbearable times. I truly believe that I was protected by the rightness (for me) of what I was doing. I never doubted my move to Boston, regardless of what those in my family—or outside of it—thought of me. As time has gone on and I go much deeper and change more, I continue to be blessed with this invulnerability. It seems that all my hard work has paid off.

Clearly, Be-coming means that we are becoming new and different—we are changing. At first, we are usually in unfamiliar territory. We are learning our way as we go. Not to worry, though. Once we start on this journey, we wouldn't turn back—even if we could. Some would say this takes courage. Perhaps, but in my case, my primary feeling is the deepest gratitude for the chance to grow and change—to Be-come more fully who I am.

SOME POEMS THAT RELATE TO BE—COMING

Continuing
her interrupted self,
she thinks herself
through.

I'm sorry I
didn't know—it
had to come to me.

That you want to be
even though you don't know
you are.

To go very deep
and find
that I am alive.

I want the pleasure
of being me. Just let me
know when I am.

May I expand
to hold
more me.

There's more of me
that will
stand me in good stead.

I have come
into my own
on my own.

I was denied what
I came to want with
all of my being.

When I do the
Right Thing
the way opens up.

AND TO JOURNALING IN PARTICULAR

I have to do this.
I will disappear
if I don't.

I get so tired of
bringing forth—and
the truth heals.

Please come, new being,
and
have something to say.

AN OPEN LETTER TO A
FORMER LOVER

Y ou came to mind recently, and you came through with such strength that I decided to go to the computer and write about you. As I typed away, I was surprised how the words poured out and how easily they came. I was both smiling and weeping as I wrote, realizing how important you had been to me. I knew you had been a strong presence in my life, but you had gone the way of all my lovers—lost to the past. Now, however, with the focus of writing, you became very clear to me and almost larger than life.

Later, as I was telling this to someone who knows you, it occurred to me—out of the blue—in a flash of insight: Maybe you had been an angel! All of an instant, I was in an interesting panic. At the time, I didn't "do" angels and you, a Scorpio Chicana with an attitude that kept everyone at a distance, didn't seem to be the type. But I had this strong notion. So, with anxious embarrassment, I told the woman, to whom I was talking, what had occurred to me and asked her if she thought I was entirely too weird to have such an idea. To my stunned relief, she said, "No, not at all. Angels are usually not recognized at the time and from what I'd said about you, you fit the description." I could hardly believe my ears—she was right with me! This no-nonsense woman who has as much attitude as you and is as politically astute. I didn't expect her to have angel-awareness any more than I expected you to have been an angel! It was just too wonderful and felt exactly right.

And yet, I did wonder what you would think of all this. Until this angelic breakthrough, I would have said that both you and I would describe our relationship as nothing but uncomfortable. We were so different: Scorpio and Aquarius; Chicana and upper class Anglo; me, the mother of three, you a disgruntled daughter. Also, you saw me as the privileged one, but from my side I felt that you had a personal power I envied. You had been to the prestigious Women's Writing Center and studied with the Great Goddesses of Radical Feminist Writing. I was impressed and in awe, and compared to you I felt like a vacuous Wannabe. My privilege didn't count for anything as far as I was concerned. But for you, it was always between us and in spite of the attraction you had for me and the genuine consideration you gave me, you resented and hated it. You weren't easy and I was often intimidated by you.

That's not the way it's supposed to be with angels. Yet, as I have thought about you in this new light, I've decided that you were as good as they get. The bad times have faded and what I remember now are the absolutely solid and worthy things you said and did for me.

Let's start with some of those things you said to me. Like: "Change or die." You said it as a direct challenge—your dark, mestiza eyes boring into mine. I heard it as a new and shocking thought. Now it is the truth of my life. At a women's bar with Carole King singing "You make me feel like a natural woman," you leaned over and whispered: "Sing love songs to yourself." Those words have become the credo of my life.

Then, when I confessed to you that I was a feminist and afraid of the girls, you asked: "What about your lovers?" You had me. I could not deny that I was afraid of them, too. But you asked kindly, knowing of course that you were one of those girls. And when my last parent died, you said: "Now you're really an orphan." You said it dispassionately, knowing what I still had to learn.

What you did for me, like what you said to me, had been important at the time, but I had let them slip away. Not any more though. I love it! You wouldn't let me go without re-membering what you said and did—literally taking you in again and giving you your rightful place.

There was the time you nursed me through my one and only experience with magic mushrooms. I was having a bad, bad trip, and you stayed with me for hours—sweet and caring. You were attentive and kind and listened patiently to my frantic need to talk—mostly about my kids. You knew exactly what to do for me and you did it—leaving my dignity intact. I would give a lot to experience that kind of attention again.

Then there was the time when you took me to the curandera. You felt that I needed "fixing"—and I did—so you made an appointment for me with The Señora and told me that you would go with me. Actually, I had no qualms about going alone. I trusted you completely and I was always more comfortable in your territory than you were in mine. So I picked you up and you directed me to The Señora's house in the barrio, where we found her folding laundry. I thought she was a bit spacey but I was also fascinated and obediently followed her directions. As she began to do her magic, she turned to you and said, "I can't work on her; she has too much fear." I was so ashamed and disappointed! But she didn't give up on me completely. She fluffed my aura, which was nice and relaxing. Then she told us that she needed some things to use for a ritual in which she would find a guide for me. I was to buy $50 (a lot of money in 1979) worth of Opium perfume and several boxes of white candles. Neither one of us batted an eye, and we left The Señora's house to go downtown and shop. I can vividly remember the two of us walking down the street, headed for the classiest store in San Antonio. We were so intent on our sacred purpose that we did not feel awkward with each other or about what we were doing.

After our expensive perfume purchase at Frost's we went to a funky religious store and bought the candles. Then, like obedient girls, we took everything to The Señora. She said she would perform a ceremony soon and that she would get in touch with me to tell me what she learned in the ritual. I realized recently that the smart woman might have sold the perfume, but I wonder if she did light all the candles in her special place and perhaps spritzed them with some of the perfume. Even if she did not, the image of such a ritual is so beautiful that it is very satisfying to me. Days later, during another appointment, she told me that a beautiful blond movie star had appeared during the ritual who wanted to look after me. This was wonderful news and not at all surprising to me because I was in the process of developing a deep affinity for Marilyn Monroe. You weren't with me when she gave me this information, or at subsequent sessions when she introduced me to two other guides I still use. But I remember well that early in our relationship I had timidly told you that I needed guidance. It was a new and rather embarrassing awareness to me but you seemed to know what I meant, and said that all I had to do was ask for it. I wonder if it was then that you planned to take me to The Señora.

My last memory of you was during a poetry reading by

Gloria Anzaldúa. You had invited her to San Antonio and after she finished reading her poetry, you asked her to read "The Bridge Poem" from the book she co-edited: *This Bridge Called My Back*. You knew I loved the poem, and when she read the important and final lines, your intense eyes looked directly into mine: "I must be the bridge to nowhere but my true self. And then I will be useful." You knew then what I needed to do in order to truly live my life.

You seemed to always know what I needed, dear one, even to the point of denying me what I wanted so much—your approval and appreciation. You weren't the first or the last to withhold them from me but with you the memory is more valuable and it doesn't hurt. Maybe that's because I asserted myself and hung up on you the last time we talked—when I had tried once again to get from you what you would not give.

And now, so many years later, I can't find you. I wanted you to know about this angelic understanding and appreciation of you. I tried every information source I could think of, including Gloria Anzaldúa, but you are not to be found. Maybe that's the way it is supposed to be. You did your magic—your rough magic—and then you left me to get on with my life.

How like an angel, my dear.

MRS. RAMSEY AND ME

R ight after my mother died, I talked about her with a friend who edited the feminist journal, *Trivia*. She exclaimed: "Your mother was Mrs. Ramsey!" At the time, I didn't know who she was talking about. Now I feel that I know Mrs. Ramsey intimately. She is the main character in Virginia Woolf's novel *To the Lighthouse* and getting to know her has made me think about myself and some things about me that I might never have thought about had I not met her—and which I <u>needed</u> to think about.

One of them is about being an "hysterical extrovert"—someone who is unconsciously and compulsively outgoing and bound to others. Freud coined this term, and because I rejected all he said about women, I stayed in denial about this survival behavior that I had learned as a child. I became this way in order to handle a deep and lonely emptiness plus the lack of a meaningful purpose—and I learned how to be an "hysterical extrovert" from my mother. As I studied Mrs. Ramsey, I began to see this way of being as the personality disorder it is and to work my way out of it and in the process to come to a loving understanding of my mother.

Mrs. Ramsey is a woman who is for others; her husband, her children, those who gather around her and those less fortunate. She is adored and fixated upon by her family and those she entertains at her table. They are charmed by her and they rely on her. In the novel, Mrs. Ramsey is compared with the character of Lily Briscoe, an independent, intentionally unmarried young artist. Lily is one of those who idealize Mrs. Ramsey and she says of this object of her adoration: "So, boasting of her capacity to surround and protect, there was scarcely a shell of herself left for her to know herself by. All was so lavished and spent." I was stunned by these words—they reminded me so much of my mother. Only once did she admit to me that her charming and attractive behavior exhausted her, but as I assumed this same way of being, I realized that she must have felt that way most of the time.

As I continued to think about Mrs. Ramsey, I realized that exhaustion is only one of the sad effects of being an "hysterical extrovert." Another one is that we are alienated from those for whom we put out so much. In the deepest recesses of my being I had known that I felt a huge distance between me and those I attracted. Sometimes I even wondered if it was because of the smoke screen of charm and compassion that I exuded, but I couldn't acknowledge or do anything about any of this because I truly didn't know any other way to be with others. I was neither grounded nor "in my body," as they say, because I was, essentially, afraid of these people. Hence: "*hysterical* extrovert." I certainly did not know myself, but those whom I had attracted and for whom I put out so much felt that I wanted to know them. In truth, what I really wanted was to be known by them. That was out of the question, since I hadn't a clue as to who I was and it's just about impossible to be known if you don't know yourself. Whose version of you are you going to believe if you have nothing to compare it with? So there was no real connection between me and those I attracted to me. Thinking about Mrs. Ramsey and her relationships became a major reason for me to want to get to know myself more deeply and more truthfully. I had begun this process before I met Mrs. Ramsey, but I had surely not finished it; I had only brushed the surface, really.

And I realized how hard it is to change from being an "hysterical extrovert." I wrote in my journal: "Mrs. Ramsey needs to take her finger out of the machine." I meant by this that her way of being had her in its grip and that she would have to *intentionally* extricate herself. I knew this because I had had to take my finger out of the machine—one that was exactly like Mrs. Ramsey's. I, too, was caught up in being very aware of others, while unconscious of my self. I would have said I was *self conscious*. Actually, I was overly conscious of how *they* were seeing me or how they felt I was seeing them. Some one once told me that I didn't know the forces operating on me. It took many, many years of self contemplation and work to both realize my self and to know what those forces were. For Mrs. Ramsey to do what I did is hard to imagine. She had no one encouraging her to examine her life and to make changes in it, even if she had wanted to. And she never had enough time— she was too available! I had the words of feminist writers telling me that I had a *right* to know myself and to take the time to do it. Even then it took many, many years of virtual solitude to build up an alternative to being an "hysterical extrovert." Getting to know Mrs. Ramsey made me give myself a lot of credit; it's an incredibly difficult persona to let go of.

Another thing I learned from thinking about Mrs. Ramsey was what was going on with my mother and grandmother when they were adored by younger women. I had observed this as I grew up and never thought it would happen to me. Of course, it did, and then I *had* to think about it and how to fix it. I hadn't gotten very far until I read *To the Lighthouse*. It was thinking about the relationship between Lily Briscoe and Mrs. Ramsey—Lily's adoration and idealization of Mrs. Ramsey—that made me realize what the problem was. It does nothing for the object of adoration. It permits her to keep on being alienated from herself and her admirers and it honors and draws on her unconscious and self-sacrificial nature, thus perpetuating it. The mentor relationship can be like this, too. The mentor thinks she's got "it" and the mentored associates what she wants *with the mentor*. She doesn't realize that she's got what she wants within herself—just waiting to be discovered and developed. Without this adoration and idealization of the older woman or the mentor, it can be as Mary Daly says: "Erratic women weave our lives, our works, not as imitations of models, or as models for others, but as unique, diversified creations." The older woman and the younger woman can see themselves as complete and original. Then they can have a give <u>and</u> take relationship. We can learn from each other and don't have to *settle* with being adored or adoring. Of course, neither Mrs. Ramsey, nor Lily Briscoe, nor my mother, nor my grandmother nor the young women who idealized them, could get to this understanding. They never *thought* about it. I was able and eager to think about it and to come to a way of changing it.

The value and *necessity* of "thinking about it" is something else I learned from my consideration of Mrs. Ramsey. She could be pensive but she was always vulnerable to being interrupted because she was so *available*. By the time I met her, I was thinking about *everything* most of the time, but I had never thought *about* this thinking. Now I realize how precious it is and how indispensable it is to my growth and change. Sometimes I have compared it to praying or meditating. It's when I get really heavy, deep and real. It's when I go to and stay with a hard truth. It's when I am able to *imagine* an alternative. Thinking can be transformative, in this sense. And it is in this sense that we can come up with a way to take our finger out of the machine. Mrs. Ramsey couldn't be left alone long enough to even approach the truth of her life much less how to change it if she had wanted to.

Maybe that's why some women in trouble stay so busy. If we take enough time to think about our life we may have to acknowledge that it isn't good or right or healthy or satisfying. Most essentially, we may have to become a priority to our selves. We may have to honor ourselves enough to listen to our true selves. And if we get this far we may decide that we want to do something about the conditions of our lives—make changes. What if Mrs. Ramsey had acknowledged to herself that she didn't care about Mr. Ramsey or any of the other people in her life *that* much? What if she entertained the thought that she was not happy—that she couldn't handle looking after everybody *any more*? What if she realized that she was living a lie? What if she began to feel that she was a mess of mistakes and didn't understand why she did as she did? What if she realized that she was caught up in a life that felt toxic and that she wanted out of it? What if she desperately wanted to change? Who would understand her or support her?

If Mrs. Ramsey and my grandmother and my mother had been *encouraged and enabled* to think about their lives and the quality of their lives, they might have had a different story. As I have said, I had the words of feminist writers urging me to know myself and to take myself seriously. I well remember reading and *hanging onto* these words of Adrienne Rich: "There are times in life when we must take ourselves more seriously or die." I also got so much from these words of Hannah Arendt: "... [If] you want to think, you must see to it that the two who carry on the dialogue be in good shape, that the partners be *friends*. The partner who comes to life when you are alert and alone is the only one from whom you can never get away, except by ceasing to think." I wanted that partner so much that thinking became invaluable to me—it was a way to get to my Self and then to have a relationship with her. By the time I was able to do this I had taken my finger out of the machine so that I was able to *be* alert and alone.

I have wished most poignantly that I could *save* all the Mrs. Ramseys of the world. Of course, I can't. But I can keep thinking about my life—how it is going and how I want it to be. And, metaphorically speaking, I can be grateful to Mrs. Ramsey for showing me the consequences of not doing this.

THE GREAT SPECULUM EPISODE

When I taught an "Introduction to Women's Studies" class at a small women's college in 1988, the syllabus included an essay by Nelle Morton entitled "Beloved Image," from her book *The Journey Is Home*. In it she describes a film made by Emily Cullpepper called "Period Piece" in which Emily films her cervix, having inserted a speculum, and lit the deep passageway with a bright light. She is menstruating and the camera records a drop of blood coming out of the cervix. The film was first shown at an Academy of Religion meeting in 1976.

This use of a speculum on one's self was not new or shocking to me because when I went to the Goddard Cambridge Graduate School for Social Change in Boston in 1975, the director of feminist studies suggested, at our first meeting, that we look at our cervix by using a speculum, mirror and flashlight. She said, holding up a plastic speculum, which she took out of her shirt pocket: "It's a spiritual experience." I believed her, and as soon as I could get a speculum at Planned Parenthood, I had my experience. I loved it. I saw a part of me that had been medicalised and mystified but which was deeply *me*. After that I gave speculums as gifts.

Also, at this time, some Women's Studies departments were talking about the procedure (now referred to as a vaginal self examination) and demonstrating it. Usually, this was not well received by their administration, which considered it too personal and not academic. But, by this time, the saying "The personal is political" had taken hold, as well as the belief that women's personal lives were the stuff of the classroom. This was the position I was coming from when I taught "Beloved Image" in 1988.

After my class read the essay, one of the students asked if I could get a copy of the film and show it. I called Emily Cullpepper and she graciously sent a copy of the video. But before I showed it, I talked about it with the head of the Women's Studies department. (From now on I refer to her as X.) She recalled how meaningful it had been in the 1970s to witness the demonstration of the exam and we decided that we wanted to show the film and do a demonstration of the procedure. She would talk about the history and significance of the self examination and demonstrate it herself. We notified students, medical personnel at the college and any women in the community who might be interested. I got plastic speculums from Planned Parenthood to give to the women after the event so that they could see for themselves.

We had good attendance and although all were not enthusiastic, many were. Most of the older women were probably nonplussed and didn't say a word but the students were, on the whole, impressed. No one at the time expressed hostility or disapproval. But shortly thereafter, X and I were summoned to the president's office.

There we were confronted by a small group of women

from the administration. They were stern and disapproving. None of them, except for the school nurse, had been present at the event. X and I both read statements in support of our action. The school nurse read a statement of her response and in it there was absolutely no understanding of what the experience meant, historically or personally. The president's response to what we said was simply, "This is totally bizarre!"

What had changed from the time when the vaginal self exam was described to me and others as "spiritual" and this meeting where it was described as misguided and "bizarre"?

For one thing, a backlash to feminism had occurred. What had been liberating and inspiring to me and to many women now seemed too personal or extraneous. What had been empowering was now embarrassing. Many women now seemed afraid to share personal experiences—ones that many of us had discussed and honored in Consciousness Raising groups.

What had made them afraid or embarrassed? I think it was not only the backlash of a patriarchy that was threatened by the personal empowerment of women; it was also the fact that the collective strength of women who had experienced that empowerment and consciousness did not hold in the face of misunderstanding and disapproval. Consequently, we lost each other's intimate support. Also, many feminists now sexualized a woman's experience so that empowerment had more to do with sexual activity than with a personal evaluation of sexuality itself. In respect to the vaginal self examination, it seemed irrelevant and women's liberation was not so much about knowing ourselves intimately as it was about expanding our sexual behavior. Of course, many of us had had just about enough of sex. We wanted to know what else we could do and we cared more about how sex hurt women than with how useful it could be. We continued to be political around such issues as sexual harassment, rape, domestic abuse and abortion. But, more and more, these issues were known as women's issues, not feminist issues. Fewer and fewer women were identifying as feminists. But there are still those of us who honor the title and see it as a description of the consciousness that brought us to where we were and see it as the name of what brought us to whatever serves us now. For many of us, what had happened to ourselves and to many women was something like "spiritual." We had found a very deep and neglected part of ourselves that we grew to be proud of. We found the *truth* of ourselves.

So it was with The Great Speculum Episode. X and I were impassioned feminists. The Movement had *moved* us and we wanted to share one small part of it with other women. The vaginal self exam represented an expression of "Our Bodies; Our Selves," which meant a discovery and a consciousness of the most personal within us. We were enabled to see ourselves *for* ourselves. This felt truly feminist to us.

As I wrote this chapter, I talked about it to a couple of younger women. One, a woman who cuts my hair, had never heard about the vaginal self exam, but said she would love to do it. The other, my acupuncturist, said she had done it after reading *Our Bodies; Ourselves* and that it had been interesting. Now, after hearing me talk about the historical and existential significance of it, she thought she might try it again. Before, it had seemed sort of clinical; now it might be more meaningful. My stylist picked up on the idea of looking at her cervix while she is menstruating. Then she began to talk about all the issues around menstruating that she had heard from her mother. I realized that examining ourselves in this way was not a dead issue.

Also, I realized in talking to both these women how important it is to not idealize either the cervix or menstruation. Before I had talked to my acupuncturist, I had visited with a man who was a massage therapist at her work place. He was reading a book about the "Men's Movement." I said that I objected to its inference that men needed to get more in touch with their "manhood." He didn't get what I meant until I said that it was like white people being encouraged to get more in touch with our "whiteness." Then, when I was talking to my acupuncturist, I realized that I didn't want women to see the vaginal self exam as a way to become *more of a woman*. And when I talked to my stylist about menstruation, I knew that I felt the same way about that. Feminism is not about idealizing or essentializing who women are or what we do; it is about asking us to examine the myths about who we are and what we do. It is about discovering the real truth about our selves. It is about seeing for ourselves.

So if you want to have this particular experience, go to Planned Parenthood and get a plastic speculum. Then get a strong flashlight and a mirror. Sit on the floor, spread your legs and insert the speculum. It might help to lubricate it with vaginal jelly, such as you would use with a diaphragm. Once the speculum is inserted and held open, shine the flashlight in through the opening and hold a mirror so that you can see your cervix reflected in it.

Hopefully, this will not only be an interesting sighting for you but a deeply meaningful experience as well. Perhaps, a truly feminist one. And then, if this very personal experience makes a particular sense to you, you will go on to see how political it is—as with so many aspects of your personal life. And then, perhaps, we can go on with our Movement.

IF A TREE FALLS IN
THE FOREST . . .

There is a conundrum that asks: If a tree falls in the
forest and there is no one there to hear it fall, does
its fall make a sound? When I first heard it, it seemed
a compelling consideration. Recently, however, I realized that it is
simply wrong thinking—no witness is needed to verify any part of
a tree's process.

However, in mid-life, when I was trying hard to find me, I got
caught up in similar questions: If I am not seen, do I exist? Or more
specifically: If no one sees me as I *really* am, how will I ever know
who I really am? Or if *they* don't notice what is within me, how do I
know I've got it, whatever it is? If my parents had no reason for my
being, how will I know that I have one now? Or if no one has ever
known what to do with me, how do *I* know what to do with me? Or if
no one valued me, how do I know my value? And if no one wanted
to hear from me, how will I know that I have something to say?

Answering these questions finally became a matter of life or
death. When I realized that I was lost to myself—that I did not feel

real to myself—I found that I literally could not live without getting to me. I had to know that I *was*—that there was someone *in there* and that it was me. And I had to do this whether anyone else cared about, or acknowledged, what I found. Before, I had placed all verification of my being outside of myself. Now, I had to come up with knowing my reality for myself. Real-izing me became my life's work.

First, I tried to figure out why I felt so lost and unreal to myself—what was going on, and how I felt about it. As I thought about it, I realized that the reason I was lost to myself and didn't feel real was that, as a child, I had disappeared. I had disappeared and become a performance. With the wisdom and brilliance of a survivor, I had learned to perform perfectly so that no one would kill me. (Of course, they wouldn't have actually killed me, but I'm sure that as a child, I felt in an unknown part of me, that they would have if I was anything but what they could handle.) So, to stay safe, I disappeared myself so that I could be acceptable to them. And *they* were everywhere.

When I couldn't live this way any longer—when I couldn't handle pretense any more—I, at first, believed there was No Exit, and I attempted suicide. But then I had a breakthrough. I didn't have to leave my life; I had to leave life as I knew it. I had to be alone. I had to literally start over and discover first that I *had* a Self and then what to do with me. As I did this, I was in free-fall and there was no one to lead me through the void. I was on my own. And that was the way I wanted it.

During this time, I read a lot. Alice Miller, the German psychoanalyst who writes so well about childhood trauma, was one writer I read with close and terrified attention. Her book, *The Drama of the Gifted Child*, explained to me why I had disappeared. She says that a child has what she calls "narcissistic needs." These are the needs for respect, echoing, understanding, sympathy, empowering and mirroring. She goes on to say that if these needs are not met *accurately* by the parents, the child can not know their True Self. Fortunately, she goes on to say that if we form a false self in the absence of these needs being met, we can later go back, as it were, and retrieve or rebirth our True Selves. Many psychologists are not so optimistic, and I felt quite damned by their suggestion that someone needed to have seen me for who I was and believed in me in order for me to have survived. I could get caught up in their pessimism, but when I read Miller, I believed her. I believed that I could get my True Self back by meeting my narcissistic needs myself. This was my salvation.

There were times I digressed and tried hard to get someone else to confirm my reality, but it never worked. Partly, this was because *I* didn't know my reality. As I said in my journal: "No one is going to get me until I get me." I also believe that it is a law of the universe that we have to know and confirm our *own* reality. It is certainly what *Know the Mystery* means.

Once I realized the legitimacy and possibility of Miller's claim—that I could retrieve my essential self—I let go of her work. Her emphasis on the fault of the mother began to get in my way, for I was unable to find any usefulness in adequately blaming my mother. Also, I was a mother and couldn't handle being blamed for my mistakes. What held more weight for me, then, was the Radical Feminist reference to the Self. I was forty years into oblivion when I read the word Self in the context of feminist writing. It was my comprehension that I had a Self, as these writers described it, that enabled me to both go to the child in me and to go on from there— to find and to take responsibility for the vision to which I was born. Miller showed me what part of the problem was; Radical Feminism gave me a richer notion of what Self seeking and Self Be-coming could be. It did not, of course, do the hard work for me. Again and again, I had to do it for my Self. And the good news is that this is not only right action, it is doable.

What I have learned as I go on and on with the process of Self Be-coming is that it takes acute desire and intention. I had to want to come into Being more than anything else. I had to want to see my Self more than I wanted to <u>be</u> seen. I had to learn that my reality and my value and my purpose depended on nothing outside of myself.

In other words, the realization that the tree falls—regardless—and existentially, that we are not dependent on being perceived in order to Be, gets us off the hook of looking to others for confirmation of our reality. It also makes us dig for what that reality is. We are in <u>our</u> hands, and our love for, and desire for, ourselves is what fuels the effort. It was with astonishment and the deepest gratitude that I wrote in my journal, recently: "I brought myself into being by wanting me."

In trying to figure out what's going on when others do not see us for who we sense we are, it may be necessary to separate from them. This is either because they need for us to see *them*, or have become attached to seeing us the way we have been. It's not so much that they refuse to see us, they simply look straight through us without seeing us. Whatever the reason, our True Selves are invisible or non-existent to them and they resist or deny or are hostile to who we suspect we are. If we want desperately enough to Be, we must get away from *having* to be seen by them for who we believe we truly are. Of course, the consequences of this separation are painful and complicated. We feel we don't *have* anybody. But we didn't have them anyway, did we? They had us! So we balance our new loneliness and emptiness with the kind we felt when we were with them. We choose the freedom and yes, sometimes the terror, of the new and the unknown.

One more thing about being seen by others is that sometimes they see in us what we have not known or acknowledged in ourselves. One consequence of this is that we are then quite confusing to them. They can't understand why we don't *know* what they see. When I realized that this was going on with me, I had to face why there was such a gap in the way I came across and the way I felt. Why did some others think I was full of a lot of "stuff" when I felt so empty? Why did they want me and I felt so lonely with them? I used to say that I felt alone amongst strangers. And I was referring to my birth and marriage families! Why did they think I had so much when I felt I had so little? Then I had to decide whether I wanted to keep any of the qualities that they saw in me—ones that they liked. As I write today, I know I've kept some of them but they feel different. I think this is because I am not trying to get attention with them or be seen because of them. I just *am*. This is a tremendous relief.

As I have become more and more real to myself, the conundrums that bothered me so much were resolved in a way that have become words of wisdom written in my little blue book of poems. As I mentioned earlier, these consist of three lines. The first is five syllables or less, the second is seven syllables or less and the third is five syllables or less. When I am writing in my journal, sometimes a thought comes through very succinctly. Then it goes into the little blue book of poems.

If they don't see it it doesn't mean it's not there.	If they don't acknowledge it, it doesn't mean they don't see it.	If no one cares, it doesn't mean it can't be-come.
"It" has nothing to do with them, so they don't (want to) see it.	They are not looking for it and wouldn't know it if they saw it.	

We _can_ deconstruct who we have become. We _can_ know who we are and what we are for. This is the sacrosanct in us, the Original Self in us. She will not let us go once we truly seek Her. She is at the beginning, in the hell of lostness and She is our destiny. She is the One who longs and the One who invites. She is the One who seeks and the One who has the answers. She is at our beginning and She is the reason for our being. She is our Alpha and Omega. She is the One who is—regardless.

THINKING ABOUT RELATIONSHIPS

...know the mystery: for if that which you seek,
you find not within yourself,
you will never find it without
—from the invocation to the Star Goddess
in *The Spiral Dance* by Starhawk
(adapted from Doreen Valiente)

For me, it is essential to be alone and to be the center of my life. It is much more important to me that I am changing internally than that I am relating interpersonally. This is not to say that I am not sensitive (sometimes overly so) to how a relationship is going. However, I have found that the times when I am changing and growing are times when I am giving very little energy to being with other people.

Of course I deal with loneliness. But I have discovered that it is much more a teacher and a healer than a condition. The more I "be with it", the more I am learning what is truly satisfying and that that is not at all what I thought or hoped it would be; i.e. someone else doing what I wanted them to do for me—preferably without my asking. What I have learned instead is that satisfaction comes from doing the vision to which I was born—to grow and to change and to do my work. I have been enticed and permitted to meet and bond with my Self and my purpose instead of looking outside myself, through traditional relationships, for what I want.

Here's how I think it has worked:

In respect to romantic relationships, I remember the ones coming after my divorce. My marriage, which lasted for over twenty years, began with attraction but became very hard to handle and is recorded in my psyche now, as a repeat of my birth family experience. Three years after my divorce, when I was 45, I came out as a lesbian. It felt easy and natural—a full circling of my feminism, i.e. that I was Self centered and woman identified. However, the relationships didn't work well for me. Not because they were Lesbian but because, as they increased in duration, they began to feel as dysfunctional as my birth and marriage relationships had been. I was still caught up in patterns that I had learned almost fifty years before, and never un-learned. When I realized this, after four years and several relationships, I chose to be celibate, believing that my inability to relate—to my satisfaction—was something only I could fix. I had pulled away from family relationships when they became unbearable for me and I now pulled away from romantic relationships for the same reason. "Sticking it out" was not an option any more.

I was in one relationship between then and now and when it ended, I knew that there would not be another one for a very long time—possibly ever. It seemed that I had not learned a thing, except how much I had to learn—not about me in a relationship, but about bonding to myself and my life's work. As I write, I have been celibate for over fifteen years, and it is working. By that I mean that my purpose in being celibate is working. I don't think that celibacy is an end in itself; it is a means to an end. And for me, that end is, simply, to have all the energy I need to do my changes and my work. I had gotten to the point where I could not look anywhere but within me to find what I wanted and had been waiting for all my life. This is nothing but what it means to Know the Mystery. I had begun that work before I entered these relationships, but in them I was sabotaging myself every time.

Here's how the mechanics of that sabotaging process worked—for me. My longing for someone outside my self could feel so strong that I have said to myself: "I-want-someone-to-breathe-the-breath-of-life-into-me." I kept feeling that maybe *they* could make the difference—the difference I couldn't seem to make. Sometimes when I watched a romantic story on television or in a movie, I would think: "Maybe" And knowing how deep and persistent this longing was made me write in the margin of my consciousness: "Sweet Scottie! I'm glad you're alone!" Not being committed enough to my Self and my work made me long for any one who had what I thought I needed. In the past, because I didn't know what to do, I fell in love with someone who seemed to know what to do. I was absolutely enthralled with women who seemed to have a life. Whether this assessment was correct or not, I needed to experience it in order to begin to recognize that I too could have a life. The problem was that I idealized them so much that I couldn't *get to* the reality of my own self. I knew that they thought I was desirable, too, but I hadn't a clue as to why. I felt one down to every woman I was attracted to. They had something I wanted and which looked awfully good on them. But while I was so in awe of them, I did nothing to develop in me what I was attracted to in them. The relationships were, indeed, Self-destructive.

This is such a natural thing to do when we don't have the opportunity to develop our potential, or to discover that our life is self justifying. It happens to girls and women all the time. In our lostness, or boredom, or trappedness, we are set up to look outside ourselves for purpose or fulfillment—something! And we are told in what we read and what we see on TV or the movie screen that true love is possible—that we can follow our heart's desire—that we can fall in love. And, that it will only help us.

So I would enter an affair, lustily and hopefully, but basically out of neediness or boredom. There was falseness at the start. I led with my neediness and longing, but it looked like nurturance or graciousness or just plain old seduction. If I had felt at ease and equal to these others, I would not have presented such a mixed message. But I was not at ease and I did not feel equal. I appeared to be confident and I was anxious. The persona I showed was committed and impassioned, but underneath it, I did not have a life that was focused enough or adequate enough to sustain me. Maybe the most complicated contradiction was that I came across as available and I was not. I wanted most to have them—to be *had* by them and like a child, I didn't want to have to do anything. Yet I came across as bountiful—effusively so. It was an illusion, but one which others could feed on quite adequately. Then, with them as my focus (which meant my need of them as my focus), I overlooked what was wrong in the relationship. I was neither satisfied nor at ease and I was in awe of someone I said I loved. I could not bear to lose them and I was never without a feeling of awkwardness and anxiety with them. Any satisfaction I had, which was usually sexual, was ecstatic, but it was frightfully insecure. Once, after a confrontation with a fellow worker at our feminist bookstore in San Antonio, I confessed to a friend that I was a feminist and afraid of the girls. She, in her wisdom, asked me how I felt about my lovers. I said, sheepishly, that it was the same with them

How terribly sad—I was afraid of my lovers. My attraction

to them was a longing for attachment. That part was sincere. What was insincere was to call it love. I was living a lie and forestalling any growth and change on my part.

So neediness led to knottedness. I got absorbed in the intimacy (which wasn't) and sucked into all that was my unfinished business. I couldn't seem to get out of what held me so painfully. I was finding out that the more insecure I was in a relationship, the harder it was to leave it, because the relationship had become its own energy field—an agglutination of false hopes and needs that held me as though my life depended on keeping them. I had participated out of my emptiness, and my deep ignorance of my options. I had gotten in a habit—a bad habit. But deep within me I knew that if I separated, I could find that part of me that I had begun to feel and to nurture after I left my marriage. I remembered again that it was not a matter of trying harder but of changing the situation.

Clearly, many of us stay in denial about the wrongness of a relationship in order to avoid being *out there* alone. "Scratch *his* love, and you'll find *your* fear," T. Grace Atkinson said in one of her brilliant speeches, and then added: "You'll be afraid you'll die, but *your life* will be born, and *you'll* begin to be *free*." (italics, mine) In a footnote she says: "I have had more women tell me they related to this one sentence than to any other statement I have made." When I first read it, I was relating to women and I knew it applied to me as much as to the heterosexual women Atkinson was addressing.

When I think of the sadness and wastefulness of loving in order to be loved, I think of Marilyn Monroe. I actually feel a great affinity with her and am grateful for the work of Gloria Steinem who has explored those parts of Marilyn that were discounted, ignored, or misinterpreted by those who made her up. With this new image of her, I could see her as a brave young woman whose desire to be wanted began to far exceed her desire for integrity. She had too much of what was wanted by others, and because she most wanted to <u>be</u> wanted, she accepted their terms. An object of compulsive desire, she couldn't develop her true identity, which would have necessitated that she address the neglect and loneliness and abandonment of her childhood. Instead, she paid attention to what others wanted of her and stayed bound to their approval. This is dreadfully sad; it was so much less than she deserved. Steinem dedicates her book, *Marilyn,* to the "real" Marilyn as well as "the reality in us all"—a reality that I feel can not be un-covered and nurtured lest we give our full attention to our selves when it is needed. Marilyn /Norma Jean can be a mentor as we seek our authentic selves—our real selves—and be able to recognize what is or is not helpful for that.

Because of my experience, I disagree with the idea that the best way to heal the wounds of relationship is *in* relationship. Long ago I believed these words: "If two people are still growing, each is too properly selfish to be intimate. If they are afraid to be selfish, one partner will consume while the other stagnates." Later, with more experience, I added: "and it may be unclear which person is which." It had become clear to me that in an unhealthy relationship I was met by someone who was very different from me. Then we worked on each other in a way that was anything but growthful. This is why I question "trying harder." For some of us, the other one affects us too much—we have no sense of indifference or detachment. I operated on the assumptions of my beginnings, and all the self-help advice in a bookstore could not get me to do otherwise. Relationship and dissatisfaction and deprivation and anxiety were as connected for me as relationship and sex are for others. Going to a rock for water was a habit for me and, of course, an addiction.

An acquaintance once tried to turn me on to the concept of complimentarity as a benefit of being in a relationship. The example she used to explain it to me was that of the diamond and the necklace—the one without the other being incomplete. I respond to this as I do to the concept of "androgyny", i.e. that a woman is more whole and complete if she adds to her self a masculine component. I believe that I am whole *as* a woman and that I am whole as a Self. I am intrigued more, by the example of a stage performance I saw on television of John Cage performing music and Merce Cunningham dancing. Each was performing independently of the other; the music did not determine the dance movements, or vice-versa. Each performance was self-justifying— they did not provide a context for each other. So why did they perform together? Because they wanted to and because it worked, is all I can figure out. But remember, each was a virtuoso of his medium and his self.

Let me be clear that I am not grinding an ax. My feelings are not about sour grapes. Yes, I was wounded in relationship. And my task and my joy now are not about trying to get me right in relationships but about getting me right with myself. I figure that if I make sense to myself—if I feel real to myself—if I trust myself—if I know myself—relationships will or will not fall into place. They are not the goal; I am.

Now I know that when a relationship doesn't work, I need to bow to my enemy, so to speak, for it is in their *not* meeting my needs that I have another chance. It seems to be a graceful law of my life that I cannot lose myself in another without doing harm to myself. I come in need and in lust—in hunger and longing—and I leave stunned, confused and exhausted.

What about sex? Well, I'm not into it except with myself. In the past, I was certainly into it and I loved it, but for me it was *the* entanglement of a romantic relationship. When a relationship turned dull or bad, sexual satisfaction was what fooled me into thinking there was a chance.

Sexual Liberals tell us that repressed sexuality is a big problem. I think that living a lie is a bigger problem. Carol Ann Douglas, a radical feminist writer, describes a conference dominated by sexual liberals: "It was vital for everyone to engage in their chosen sexual behavior, but not so crucial for us to develop our analysis or state our opinions about sexuality." This position (that of sexual liberals) usually glorifies and eroticises difference. Even the "best" think that being in relationship with someone different is expanding because we modify our behavior or thinking in response to theirs. That's a good thing if it's mutual, but for me it doesn't work. I fell in love with people who were very different from me and I didn't expand, I shrank in the comparison. Also, it is my belief that it is manipulative to eroticize someone. I resent it being done to me, for I didn't ask for it and it feels invasive.

I particularly like what Jane Roberts says about sex in *The Nature of the Psyche*: "If children believe that identity is dependent on performance (sexual performance), then they will begin to perform as quickly as possible and society will suffer because the great creative thrusts of growing intellect and intuition will be divided at puberty, precisely when they are needed."

When I was 14 years old, I could have gotten pregnant. I was lonely and untouched (literally) in my family and sex felt like it might be *connection*. Actually, it was scary and embarrassing and when I realized that I could get pregnant, I vowed to quit having intercourse until I got married. As I have told high school students in sex education classes, that's a poor reason to get married.

So, sex has not done it for me. It is surely not about self-discovery as far as I am concerned—unless it is the discovery that what I want most is not found in a sexual encounter. The abandon that is so delicious in a sexual meeting was dreadful for me because invariably I ended up abandoning myself.

But I'll tell you what a relationship might look like in the best of all situations. I think about this when I'm challenged by someone who is intolerant of my solitude or when I am longing to be ready to leave it.

The John Cage/Merce Cunningham model looks good to me. It's like parallel play—each one knowing what they're doing and being into it. I like imagining the self-containment of each one—not caring what the other is doing but knowing that the other is doing something that they understand and respect. I like what the poet Hilda Doolittle said: "I go where I am loved and where I love—into the snow. I go to the things I love without duty or pity." I like the idea of being neither for nor against the Other. I like the advice: "Don't settle. It's better to have nothing than to have inferior something." I like believing that a free relationship is about being able to survive the experience of displeasing, defying or dissociating from the other. (Marilyn Frye, *In and Out of Harms Way*) I like directing the words of a love song to myself.

I like the ideas of Janice Raymond about Gynaffection in her book, *A Passion for Friends.* Gynaffection means: "to move—to stir—to arouse women to action—to influence and affect other women to full power." I like her concept of "two sighted seeing", something sort of like parallel play, but different in that there is a common goal in the seeing.

I also like the concept of Sparking and Spinning between women, developed by Mary Daly in *Pure Lust.* Sparking is when we ignite each other or turn each other on with our thought or action. Spinning is more leisurely, in my mind. It is when we wonder and wander in our pondering together—taking our time. In both cases, we reach a place that we might not have reached had we had not been together.

And I like Marilyn Frye's concept of the "loving eye": "The loving eye makes the correct assumption: the object of the seeing is *another* being whose existence and character are logically independent of the seer and who may be practically or empirically independent in any particular respect at any particular time."

But again and again and again, my focus is not on trying to achieve any of these types of relationships or of getting me to be able to participate in one. My focus, my desire, my deepest joy and satisfaction is growing and changing and I just can't seem to grow and change when I'm focused on maintaining a relationship. That's just the way that it is.

ORANGES AND IDENTITY

A few years ago I went to a writing workshop. When I entered the room I noticed a table piled with many objects. I figured that they were for a writing exercise. One of them was an orange. When I saw it I knew I had a topic and that I had to be the one to get it. I obsessed during the first writing exercises about how I was going to get to the orange first. Fortunately, I was close to the table and when the leader of the workshop said to go to the table and choose an object, I was up in a flash. I casually picked up the orange and was writing before she gave us our ten-minute limit. Here is what I wrote:

> Once I went to a workshop at a Holistic Health Conference. I don't remember what it was about, but in the middle of the room was a pile of oranges. We were to pick out an orange and look at it until we really knew it. After a bit we were told to put our orange back into the pile with all the others.

Then we were to go to the pile again and find our orange. I was successful; I found my orange! But then we were told to get a partner and share our orange—actually hand it to them—so that they could "learn" our orange and be able to identify it as we had. My partner was my lover at the time and when it came time to hand over my orange to her, I realized to my horror that *I could not*. I knew then that my jig was up in respect to our relationship because I could not give myself/my orange to her. I don't remember what I did to avoid giving it to her—I was too nervous—but somehow she never got it into her hands. This was a great learning experience, as they say.

I got good feedback when I read my piece, which was great, but what means the most to me is that the memory of that experience confirms what I now know with all of my being: I cannot entrust myself to another—no matter how much I long to do just that. Most importantly, it reminded me that I can trust my intuition to guide me and that I will follow it no matter how hard it is, or seemingly, how little sense it makes. Someone could have said to me: "But she was your lover! Surely you trusted her." But I didn't trust *me* enough to put myself into her hands. It felt like giving me away and I knew in my bones that I must not do that. I might not get me back! Whether anyone, including her, could understand that was not the issue. My knowing it was what was vital and it was what led me to do the right thing for myself.

Knowing when we must not hand ourselves over—when we must not put ourselves in someone's hands—is what will save us for our Selves when we need ourselves. This is anything but easy to learn, especially if we yearn to give ourselves over to someone and have them *have* us. This had been my agenda all of my life. But at the time of the orange, I had gotten close enough to my Self and committed enough to her to know when I was going against her—when I was sabotaging myself.

Before the experience with the orange I had read and *believed* these words: "When two people are still growing, they must be too selfish to become intimate, else one will consume and the other stagnate." I believe its truth influenced my inability to share my growing identity—to hand over my orange, so to speak.

The essential thing is to want to know my self more than I want someone else to know me—to have me more than I want someone else to have me. Learning how to pull this off has been a life work and I have gotten better at it as I grow and change. The blessed trick is to know who I am safe with and to know it *before* I get involved. This is doable and so well worth the effort if I want me more than anyone else. Essentially, it's freedom.

> *I saw a woman sleeping. In her sleep she dreamt Life stood before her, and held in each hand a gift—in the one Love, in the other Freedom. And she said to the woman, "Choose!" And the woman waited long; and she said, "Freedom!" And Life said, "Thou hast well chosen. If thou hadst said, 'Love,' I would have given thee that thou didst ask for; and I would have gone from thee, and returned to thee no more. Now, the day will come when I shall return. In that day I shall bear both gifts in one hand." I heard the woman laugh in her sleep.*
> —Olive Schreiner (1855-1920)

WHEN THE BOTTOM FELL OUT, I FELL TO THE BEGINNING

Some Thoughts about Menopause and Aging

I once saw a program on television about a town where most of its people were on Prozac. One woman said that she took the drug because when she menopaused, she felt that "the bottom fell out" and she couldn't handle it. I also bottomed out when I realized that I was definitely aging.

When I turned fifty, I wrote in my journal: "I don't have forever to be Scottie." This realization didn't bother me too much at the time, but later, when I menopaused, I bottomed out. Aging freaked me out. I was obsessively afraid of death and I was not ready for any of this.

My exposure to the topic of menopause was limited to two experiences. The second one was in a workshop sponsored by the publication *Our Bodies, Ourselves* in Boston. It was the mid-seventies, and for the women attending the workshop, there was a feeling that we were doing something radically new. We were *talking about* the experience of menopause with strangers. I was forty-one at the time and couldn't quite relate, but I do vividly remember a woman talking about her symptoms and how she just couldn't handle them. She said she had decided to use hormone replacement therapy. I don't remember anyone talking about another approach.

The tone and content of this workshop were very different from those in a "Purex Special for Women" that I watched in the 1960s. This program was my first experience hearing about menopause and it was all about it not needing to be such a big deal. I learned that in Europe, women did not have the dark and heavy time that I was accustomed to hearing about. This was the message I took to heart, not the one made by the woman in the workshop.

When I menopaused, I did not have hot flashes but I did have horrendous headaches and I experienced a terrible loss of energy and a deep depression. What kept me from doing hormone replacement therapy or taking antidepressants was what I had tucked away in my subconscious while watching that "Purex Special for Women" so many years before. I knew that I wanted to *consciously* get through this experience and come out intact in the end. As the I Ching says: "Persistence in a righteous course brings reward." I know now that it does.

I was not drawn to the popular ways of dealing with menopause and I read only one book. It was written by the herbalist Susan Weed. What she said was alarming but it seemed useful. She suggests that when we menopause we are going through a "melt down" and that we don't want to do this in front of people. She also says that the change we go through is *total*, like changing from being a plush easy chair to being an ordinary metal kitchen chair. I took what she said to heart and began the long haul. As I am now on the other side of this a-mazing experience I can bear witness to what Susan Weed said.

To wit:

At 50 I was in love with Hecate, the mythical, wise and indomitable old woman. Maybe I thought, or hoped, that I would now become like her—wise and indomitable. But as it had been in all my love affairs, I couldn't get what I fell in love with. In fact, as I seriously entered the process of menopausing, I lost Hecate. And everything else, it seemed. I lost interests and talents and talismans. Once I had been a master seamstress; now, I could not bear the thought of sewing. I had been very political, both in party politics and in feminist politics; now, I couldn't care enough. I had had a love affair with the Statue of Liberty that sustained me in a very real way; now I had no feeling for her. Nothing that had uplifted me worked anymore. Nor could I call up my old survival behaviors. I could not come up with enough charm to keep from disappearing. I could not seem to care about anything enough to keep me going. Who I was was not clear to me. I was in an identity crisis that was more scary and lonely than any I had faced before and what's more, I was gaining weight and I had no energy. The bottom had dropped out. I was lost, isolated, and alone—*exactly as I had felt as a child.* I wrote in my journal: "When the bottom fell out, I fell to the beginning."

The experience of an older woman feeling like she did as a child is a live one for some women. For too many years, women who had this experience were diagnosed as having "involutional melancholia." I had heard women talk about their mothers *having* it and it sounded dreadful. However, by the time I felt this way, such a diagnosis had been dropped from the medical literature, but I still felt as I had as a child—poignantly and palpably. I renamed my experience: "turning inward with sadness." I think if every woman who was diagnosed with "involutional melancholia" had been able to turn inward with her sadness and been left alone to go into the Background of her life, unmedicated, she might have gone through The Change with her Self new and intact. This is what I had the opportunity to do.

To begin with, I lived alone. I had already distanced myself from family so there was no one close at hand to be put off or frightened by my symptoms. There was only me to deal with and I was more than willing to go all the way with me – to go back through all the feelings of my childhood. I let myself feel the alienation and isolation and loneliness of that time. I talked to me. I listened. I had nothing but compassion for me. I had been here before—this place of attentive and salutary solitude—but this time had a *brutal* feeling of the unknown.

I felt no connection to, or satisfaction, in what I did. I didn't know why I was alive. I couldn't see a way out or why I had to feel so empty. I feared I would die from all this and I didn't want to die. Staying alive became my work. The only grace-full awareness was that before this time I had experienced my Self. Now I wanted her and to *be* her again, more than anything.

No one could be there for me because I couldn't be intelligible about what was going on. My kids thought they needed me, and I couldn't be there for them. That had to be okay and staying out of touch as I did, I didn't have to know what they thought about me. I wasn't completely out of touch, but when I was talking to them I was terribly uptight. I felt alone amongst strangers (an old familiar feeling) and it was nobody's fault. What I was going through was mine alone to deal with.

So the more I was alone, the better it was for me. I didn't

have to fake it when I was alone. I could identify with any change. I could "pray all day"—something which had for many years been a salutary solution for me, atheist that I am. I could take myself as seriously as I needed to and I could be totally self involved. I could deal only with this tremendous test. I was working very hard—more than I ever had—wanting just to hang in, to stay alive, and not to leave myself. I yearned with all my *being* for a future and to stay conscious. Because the effort was so intense, I decided that this time was indeed about testing my resolve to live and to have a life—to see if I really wanted myself and how I wanted to be. I had to reach to limits I was so afraid of that to even approach them made me want to run away. I was both running and reaching, but of course, my reaching was what was so remarkable. For it was truly a reaching into an unknown, yet desired, place. I had to literally *see* my way. In a sense, I had to *create* my way. This depended only on my desire and my wise Self's willingness to meet me halfway. As Marilyn Frye says: "There probably is really no distinction, in the end, between imagination and courage." I was working on both.

During this long time, I kept reading and my reading gave me two concepts that helped. One was from Carolyn Heilbrun's *Writing a Woman's Life*. It is her concept of *going through the door* of the third stage of our life. What enticed me was her suggestion that if I went through this door, I would be more productive than I had ever been before. Since I had never felt productive before, this really made me want to go through that door! I would be all *new*. Perhaps I would be wise and indomitable. Perhaps Hecate was waiting on the other side!

Heilbrun does not talk about how much effort this passage takes, but she does point out that Virginia Woolf didn't make it through. Knowing the challenges that Woolf faced, I had both compassion for her and a deep gratitude that I had a solitude in which I could heal and grow and change as well as be the only interpreter of myself.

The other concept that kept me going is from Mary Daly. She calls it the "Telic Focusing Principle." Telos (from the Greek) has to do with "an ultimate end." So telic focusing called me to focus on my purpose—my ultimate end. The purpose of my life became the focus of my life. In my case, I had to *come up* with my purpose plus the realization that I had the right and the capacity to claim it. I came to believe that the presence of the creative telos was a state of grace. and I held to that "mysterious telic centering principle within" as though my life depended on it—and it did. If I did not hold to it I felt fragmented, lost and stagnant—spiritually dead. So I worshipped at the shrine of telic focusing.

Gradually, all my hard work began to pay off and I got through menopause intact. Now I am simply aging which still pretty much freaks me out. I don't get it. I cannot believe I am the age I am. But clearly, I am. I'm healthy though, and there's a lot to think about. I still have a lot more to say to myself. So I age.

The hardest part—along with the unbelievable changes I see in the mirror—is facing death. When I first realized my mortality, I tried to figure out some way *around* it. Fantasizing that I could live forever was my favorite. But as the years add up, I have to be realistic, don't I? I had best give up the fight and figure out a way to live with the reality. And as with any reality, giving in is the only way to freedom. I'm not home free yet, but I <u>am</u> building a trust in the process of my life. This, plus my love and approval of myself, will come through for me—in the end. I'm sure of that.

Once I had a dream in which my mother died. I woke agitated and anxious, as though I were dead or dying. Then I had a blessed breakthrough—a vision, really. I was wherever it is that we go when we die and my Self was asked: "So, how was it being Scottie?" The answer was: "I loved her very much."

So Be It

CONSIDERING
DEPRESSION

If you bring forth what is within you,
what you bring forth will save you.
If you do not bring forth what is within you,
what you do not bring forth will destroy you.

—The Gospel of Thomas
from *The Gnostic Gospels*

I have heard it said that depression is an avoidance of responsibility. I disagree. I have heard it said that depression is repressed anger. That may be true, but for me, that was not what was repressed. I have heard that depression is due to a chemical imbalance. I think this is a reversal; a chemical imbalance may result from repression, but just treating a chemical imbalance will not get to the heart of the matter. It is the heart of the matter that is so important and such a gift, if you will. My experience is that there are good reasons to be depressed and that to be depressed is full of possibility. Getting through it is hard work but only the hard work pays off, because depression is a signal that feelings have built up that need to be faced and figured out. We have experienced a trauma of some kind that won't let go of us and it dread-fully wants our attention. There is no where to go but down into the pain and the confusion of it and then out of it.

I didn't experience this work as a choice; I couldn't bear not to do it. What I was doing in order to survive was killing me. The silence that surrounded my pain was screaming at me.

In this sense, depression was a gift because with it I got all of my attention. I also learned that when I felt in the most danger and the most hopeless, I was closest to a breakthrough. I then had to push harder—just keep going—in order to have that breakthrough. If I had avoided facing my fears and all of what I was feeling, I would not have been able to be-come my Self. I would have continued being an empty shell, an automaton, simply performing. But I persisted with the hard work of deconstructing and constructing myself anew. I changed. I did not die.

While we are changing, we do indeed go through the void of non-being—of not knowing who we are or what we are for. We don't know whether we'll come out of it. And when we are going through this part of the process, we are not happy. We don't smile as we did before; we are scared to death.

Other people, unless they have gone through the same experience, can become part of the problem. They don't know what to do with us and they may be frightened by our fear. They may be put off by our inability to be there for them as we were before. They may be impatient with what they see as our stuckness or weakness. They may feel guilty for not being able to understand or help. Worst of all, they may sense, but not be able to deal with, their involvement in our pain. What they want is for the situation to change, for us to just get over it and they don't want to have to do anything about it themselves. Usually they can't.

When our depression is increased by the response of

others—when we can't get to ourselves because of our affect on others—I believe that we have to separate from them in order to heal. Blame doesn't help. They are not what matters any more. Only coming to ourselves and our feelings matters and we need all of our attention. We have a long row to hoe.

In doing this we are asked for strength and trust that we do not know we have. Yet we <u>must</u> trust ourselves and our timing and we must trust our fears—ones that we think we maybe should avoid. In this sense we must follow only our own wisdom. Others have their way but it may not be ours. We must follow our own lead, seek our own unique guidance, and develop a trust and a patience that are their own reward. In the end, we will know that what was required to deal with it is part of the gift of depression.

I was lost in my depression until I started writing in a journal. The lines from the *Gospel of Thomas*, which precede this chapter, remind me again and again why journal writing is so salutary. When I "bring forth what is within" me, I release some of the tension of an awful feeling.

Here are some of my journal entries:

> Why am I so alone after working so hard?
> I want someone to care how miserable I am and
> to care enough about me to keep me alive—to
> make me want to live. I am so lonely and I don't
> know what to do or talk about and no one can do
> anything for me. The emptier I get, the more frantic
> I am. Nothing I know of now, works. I feel there's
> a barrier that is insurmountable—that I don't have
> what it takes. I want a way out that I do not know
> . . . I can't handle people and I'm lonely; I can't
> handle change and I'm bored.

The pain is unbearable. How can I go on? Where do I go? I feel so broken and freakish.

I feel like I've been here forever. Dreams are about abandonment, being ignored, rejection. There is nothing new.

This is unbelievably hard and I don't like it. I cannot feel myself. Will I survive? I feel weak and vulnerable—I don't trust and I don't want to get better. I'm too tired to try any harder.

Having nothing—not knowing I have anything and not wanting to give up, is exhausting. I want to be with myself and that self is suffering so much now. What does it take to be willing to live and not just endure?

My reason for being is not as strong as my fear of losing it. I spend my day running—afraid of losing desire. I am just moving with every desire as though it is a life-line—not knowing what to do and wanting so much to want to do something.

All these words were lifted directly from my journals, starting with 1983 and I could have gone back to 1964 when I started journaling. I was thirty years old then and my entries were like those of a child. The words came out halting and awkward and there were very few of them. They were like stabs in the dark. But I gathered steam and once I got familiar with myself and my feelings, I was more articulate about them. When I began, all I could say was how unhappy I was. Just that. Later, I would be able to give content to that unhappiness. I would be able to say that I was unhappy because . . . As I did this I had to keep on with what ever feeling came up until it was recognized, even loved. I could not hate or deny or judge any feeling I felt. They wanted to be known. They had been waiting for my attention ever since I'd been born. The only thing I had to do was just keep on keeping on with them.

I do believe that it is imperative for us to know the causes of our depression so that we do not blame ourselves. This process is about consciousness and understanding; it is not for the purpose of finding who to blame. It is about acknowledging the trauma that happened to us and its consequent feelings, whether they started with our birth or later. It is about being in our truth and that truth making us free.

In my case, I found that I had been dependent on an inadequate source. I had been going to a rock for water since I was born. I realized that I had been denied and abandoned because I was dangerous to my parents who did not know how to handle their own unhappiness or fear or discontent. They could not understand or validate me since they could not understand or validate their own existence. So I became what they <u>could</u> handle and how they wanted me to be. I began to live their lie and gave up wanting to be seen for myself or to be heard. I performed. I disappeared. I became depressed.

With the reading of Alice Miller (specifically *The Drama of the Gifted Child*), I saw that I had had to suppress the trauma of my childhood in order to protect both myself and those who could not or would not acknowledge how they affected me. I knew that I had endured many years of denial, locked into vicious cycles of repetition. I had begun by being pressured to not feel or express my feelings. As I denied or hid my emotions, I began to lose touch with this soul-full part of me. I kept getting into horrid messes that proved to me that it was dangerous to be emotionally aware and honest. I was afraid of what I could not please. I was uneasy with performing but it was all I had learned to do in order to survive. I performed and I left me behind. I believed that what hurt me could obliterate me and that I either had no capacity to change this or that it was way too hard to try. I recognized the truth of Mary Daly's words: "For, since those kept in a state of being inaccessible to themselves feel worthless, self-sacrifice is a logical conclusion to their condition."

This is the terrible split, which I believed was irrevocable and would preoccupy me fruitlessly and destructively until I did something about it. In order to do that, I first had to give it all the attention that it needed. I nursed it along, understanding it more and more, not judging it but hearing it out until it was ready to open. During this process, it was imperative to handle myself with a tenderness that I had never known. I had to realize that I had done nothing wrong. I had simply survived. But I also had to come up with an alternative. I had to find my True Self. I had to real-ize that I was at the heart of the matter.

There are certainly times when I am still depressed—sad and scared. They don't last long now because I know that I will get through—if I give it everything I've got.

Here are some other things that I did as I went through my depression:

I was always honest with myself and I trusted myself and my timing. No one knew better than I what I needed and what I was about. I did know when I was, and when I was not, on the right track.

I learned the difference between what I knew was for me and what was not. This took time and patience. I was learning discernment—something graciously new.

I felt the feelings and I stayed with them as much as I could. I learned, finally, that I would come through. This took determined persistence and a gathering trust that change could happen.

Others often recommended drugs. Sometimes I wondered if this was for my sake or theirs. I did use anti-depressants for a very short time, twice, but at that time, I was not doing the hard work that I have talked about. I was not giving "it" all that I had. Now I know that only my hard work has paid off.

I had to learn to stop and endure the silence, to drop down into the void, to the heart of the matter, and remember that, oddly enough; I was there—waiting for me.

I began to realize that nothing new would come from trying to make it happen. Once I wrote: "I can't make it happen, but I sure can receive it." I had to imagine what I wanted and then wait. I kept saying these words of Mary Daly: "The courage to create is the courage to summon out of the apparent void, new being." It would help to acknowledge that it was an *apparent* void.

I found that emptiness could lift by emptying. Sometimes a huge cry left me feeling whole. It took really feeling a feeling to start me crying.

When I could, I honored all the strength that this work was taking. Breaking through the old and the familiar is an a-mazing effort!

I gave myself permission to recognize and leave toxic situations. This is clearly something many children know to do, but which some of us must learn to do as adults. I kept remembering something John Hartford (the musician) said: "They say, whoever they are, that when you quit giving a damn to whoever you're supposed to give damns to, that that's when it, whatever it is, begins to happen."

I began to not worry about being "self involved." In my case, it was a good thing. I didn't want to get out of myself; I wanted to stay inside myself.

I learned not to compare. As a therapist said to me once: "Scottie, when your life is over, you won't be asked how much like someone else you became but how much like yourself you became."

I believed that I didn't have to do anything I couldn't. I would hold the thought though and then later I might find that I was able to do whatever it was. Maybe not.

And finally, I don't "should" on myself.

In closing, I want to say that I believe and know by the way that I know, that my unique and precious self is in the midst of, and at the end of, this experience we call depression. She is so worth the time and the effort that I give to Her. She had been waiting for me all of my life and She waits for me now.

MOM'S JUST OUT
THERE TRYING TO
BREAK THE GRID

In 1976 I picked up a copy of the magazine Women and Art and saw a picture of a painting entitled "Mother's just out there trying to break the grid." I changed "Mother" to "Mom" and those words have been above my desk ever since. I didn't get the name of the artist so I simply thank her, whoever she is.

I have a compulsion, perhaps a *calling,* to defend mothers when they are being feared or hated or blamed or discounted or disdained or whatever puts them down—even 'bad mothers' who wound or abandon or even kill their children. When a mother doesn't do it right, or even does it wrong or is perceived as not doing it right, I try to understand why.

This is not easy to do when I am with the women (Why is it almost always women?!) who are telling me how awful or inadequate their mother was—how controlling, mean, and unloving she was or how boring, inept and pathetic she was. It seems I am on the wrong side when I feel for her. But I persist. I care deeply about these mothers, for I know that they have lost their way and I desperately want them to come to their lives/their Selves even when they think there's no way or no use or no time left—especially when they think no one cares or understands.

I do know that there are women who become mothers consciously and who do it well and contentedly. I am not concerned about these women. I speak about those women who mothered with non-awareness, a vague confusion or blatant discontent and who are not happy. I realize that many, if not most, of these women would deny that there's a problem with their experience of mothering. I imagine, however, that there are some who know that they are discontented with the experience and that they have lost something in the process. Probably, they don't want to admit this to themselves because they feel helpless and hopeless about changing it. Perhaps, they don't feel that their life is worth saving—that *they* are worth saving. But I know that they are and that they can be reborn to themselves, finally.

So what follows is for these women. I am hoping to shine a light on what has been unacknowledged or felt as vague "bubbling ups." I speak from my own experience alone, and what I offer is the result of many years of hard work and lots of thinking and writing. And of course I speak to you who have never thought about mothers like these who seem so unnatural and/or just plain bad. My hope is simply that I raise your consciousness about the role of mothering—a role that I think has been so ill conceived and radically misunderstood. If I do so, I am glad.

So how do a mother's problems start? Well, too often many of us become mothers when our own dependency needs were never met—essentially, when we were never loved or wanted. This results in a deprivation—an Absence—that reproduces itself when we become mothers to our children. We begin by believing what we are told and want desperately to believe—that we can get the love we want by giving it to someone else, especially our children. We don't know what to do for ourselves, so we do for them (and probably all others) what is expected, unconsciously hoping that it will meet *our* needs and that we are doing the right thing. In so doing, we are completely in the dark, for we have no idea that our emptiness and our not knowing (even our wrongdoing) are really the result of our Self longing for itself. We "mother" off the top, and our essential Self goes on hold.

Actually, this arrangement *shouldn't* work. To ask an unSelfconscious woman to mother is like asking an unconsciously frightened man to be a marine. We can perform but we are not truly *there*. A constructed self is there—a self that can be used. Of course, when a person is being used, it is essential that they *not* know what's going on or what they are truly for. In the mother's case, her performance can look either "good" or "bad," but I believe that if you asked her what she would rather be doing, she would have no idea what that might be. Maybe she would. But if she does, I doubt that she has any idea as to how she could get away from where she is to where she wants to be. She is a woman torn apart by not knowing.

When I was actively mothering, I wrote in my journal: "They want me to do things for them that were never done for me, like listen and understand and care and support. The problem is that I *can* do these things without ever having received them. I do them in some strange, unknown way in order to *experience* them or to have them come back to me. The awful part is that I have gotten so good at doing them that they look *natural*. I seem to be naturally endowed with what they want and need. And yet *I am not*."

At this point, I was experiencing a spiritual crisis. I had

committed spiritual suicide. A spiritual death results from putting others first when we are empty—from trying harder when we are at a loss. Self sacrifice is soul loss when we have no Self. In my case, I did the best I could and it did *me* no good. It did not build my ego, it did not keep me from being suicidal, and it did not give me a sense of what I was truly for. Essentially it was an experience from which I had to heal, just as I was healing the experiences of *my* childhood. As I did this, I felt no blame or shame. I only knew that I had a lot of work to do.

The Sins of Unconscious Mothering

A wise person said to me once that "to sin" means "not to know."
It is this meaning that I use here.

Some say that the sins of the fathers are visited on their children. This is a true statement and is acknowledged by sons and daughters who testify to the abuse or neglect or abandonment of their fathers. They speak of him with disgust or hate or dismissal, but I don't believe that there is any resentment like that felt by a son or a daughter toward their mother for *her* abuse, neglect or abandonment. It seems that there are no sins like those committed by the mother. Why is this? Is it a belief that if women aren't "naturally good", there will be no goodness in the world and no one will be taken care of? Goodness knows, we are dependent on our mother and we want her and we need her. But if she is not *really* there, if she is living a lie, she will pass on to her children her own sins—her own not-knowing.

What might the "sins" be that are passed on by unconscious mothering? I am going to pose these as questions and there are a lot of them.

For starters, what about the mother *needing* but not *wanting* a child? Doesn't that put the child in the position of meeting *her* needs? Won't there always be denial and mixed messages in their relationship? Does her capacity to live a lie (pretend that she wants what she didn't intend) teach us how to live a lie?

Can you, as the child, be the center of your own agenda, if you were the center of your mother's agenda? Can you be free? Can you have a reason for being if you know that there was no good reason for you to be born? Do we forget that we have forgotten that we were an accident? Do we tolerate "non-sense" because the non-sense of our conception is too confusing or painful to deal with? When our conception doesn't make sense, do we struggle the rest of our lives to make sense of our life? Because our mother didn't know what to do with us, do we have a hard time knowing what to do with ourselves? If our mother made the best of a bad deal, is that a part of our cellular learning? Does "making the best of a bad deal" then become part of the human condition?

Can our mother meet our emotional needs if hers were denied, and if she could not meet our emotional needs, do we find that ours can never seem to be met by those with whom we are in relationship? If she didn't know how to have a healthy and mutually satisfying relationship with us (or anyone else), do we become addicted to unhealthy relationships? Are we terrified of losing another because we never *had* her? Because she could not know what she truly wanted, do we have a hard time knowing what we want? If she was empty and deprived, do we have a tendency to feel empty and deprived? Does her existential loneliness become ours? Because she had no sense of her own separateness, do we have trouble with boundaries? If she had no sense of the vision of her life, do we have no sense of ours? Because she became part of the cycle of abuse or neglect, are we resigned to that cycle?

And in respect to all these "sins" of the mother, whose problem is it?

Most of the time, if not nearly all of the time, it is said that they are the mother's problem that the child inherited. I would agree. But whose problem gets our concern? Usually, if not always, it is the child's. I believe that this is so because everyone has had a mother, but not everyone has been a mother. It is hard to identify with someone's experience if you have never experienced it and/or if you are on the other side of a bad relationship with them. Also, it seems that the child is the important one to consider because they are the innocent victim in the relationship. But did the problem *originate* with the mother? Did she *invent* her "sins"? Is it like she had a germ that her child *caught?* I believe not. But in this case she does seem to be the perpetrator. So what do we do with her? Do we just ignore her or dismiss her with the proper blame—adequately discount her after naming her abuse or her total inadequacy? This is what is usually done by therapists and in the media. But could we change this and feel an equal concern for this woman who so desperately needs it in order to heal and to find her life? Could we see her as one who is *as important* as her children? This, of course, is what I am advocating.

The Oppression Of Mothers As Women, Or: What Does Misogyny Have To Do With The Concept And Experience Of Mothering?

Are these statements true of women in general, or mothers in particular?

It is assumed that what is good for her is what's good for you. Her reason for being is to facilitate yours. There's no one who can do this like she can. No one else is as understanding and gentle as she is. There's no one who listens like she does.

She feels trivialized, demonized, romanticized, or idealized.

She will put herself down before someone else can. She will stifle herself so as not to be called controlling or unfeeling or self centered or demanding or threatening or mean.

Because she couldn't win, she just gave up and behaved.

If she breaks down due to weariness or a broken spirit, she is deemed weak and/or selfish and is ignored and cast out.

If she acts for herself and it goes against another, she is called controlling, unfeeling, self centered, selfish, unnatural and is ignored and cast out.

She is either for you or against you.

Again, are these statements about women in general, or mothers in particular?

Adrienne Rich has this to say about herself as a mother in her landmark book, *Of Woman Born*: "I committed myself to an outward serenity and a profound inner boredom. If boredom is simply a mask for anxiety, then I had learned *as a woman*, to be supremely bored rather than to examine the anxiety underlying my Sistine tranquility." What could that anxiety be *for a woman*? Could it be the denial of the vision to which she was born—either not knowing that she has one, or believing that she does not qualify for one? Perhaps she senses that there <u>is</u> a vision to which she was born but can't imagine how to commit to it? Or could her anxiety be a vague sense that with every act of understanding and love for others, she moves further away from the unloved child within her—that with every cry she goes *to*, her own uncried cry is once again ignored or denied? Does she know somehow that everything is on hold for her? Does she overvalue others because there is no other way to relate? And, what's more, does she believe that such a way of relating is all that makes her real or good or valuable? Simply put, could her anxiety be that she does not have or know or value her true self?

But what's a mother to do? Adrienne Rich says: "It is as if the suffering of the mother, the primary identification of woman as mother, were so necessary to the emotional grounding of human society, that the mitigation or removal, of that suffering, that identification, must be fought at every level, including the level of refusing to question it at all."

As a woman who became a mother, why would I have ever set myself up for such service and sacrifice, with their consequent anxiety, if I had known it would be that way and that I must just suffer in silence? I didn't know I would be a "failure." I didn't *mean* to "sin." I certainly did not set out to be an *unnatural* woman. I simply accepted my pregnancy as a given and then got on with the program.

The Bad Mother

A friend once said to me: "But there <u>are</u> bad mothers!" My response was: "For good reason."

In respect to "bad mothers," I realize that it is a challenge to support a mother who is in a hellish mess and has seemingly created it, but for me it's worth the effort for *these are my people.* I care about them. I've been there. Not everywhere that they've been. I've never been on the street. I've never been poor. I've never been hooked on anything that would bring relief or some pleasure. But I do feel deep affinity for women who, for no fault of their own, are "bad mothers."

Some of these women come across as powerfully self willed and self centered. But this is not the self-centeredness I am talking about, which allows a woman to mother consciously and with satisfaction. These "bad mothers" are control freaks, often abusing what they cannot control. And because they cannot control their life, or some enterprise more appropriate to them than mothering, they compensate by over-controlling their child. The sad consequence is that they share with their seeming opposite (the empty and wishy-washy mother) an incapacity to perform the duties of mothering and come out fulfilled. It's a bad deal for everyone. And a very sad thing is that mothers and their critics can believe that *as a mother,* she does not need to be fulfilled. The argument here is that the capacity to give without needing to receive is part of the mother's job description and that, if she doesn't like this arrangement, she shouldn't have gotten into it. But she did get into it, for whatever reason, and the result is an escalating and horrific drama. She didn't "ask for it" and she's got it. And we give her a very hard time.

There is a particular demonization, I think, in our bad-mother bashing. Why do we not look on her as one of us gone wrong— unintentionally? Why can't our goal be to not place blame but to figure out why these women "went wrong" and found themselves on the wrong path?

In her book, *For Your Own Good: Hidden Cruelty in Child-*

Rearing and the Roots of Violence, Alice Miller includes a look at Hitler's past to show the roots of his sadism. She has paragraphs more to say about why Hitler did as he did, than she does about why her own mother did as she did in practicing "poison pedagogy" on her. She dismisses her mother cursorily, with a brief description of how she operated and an equally brief consideration of why she behaved as she did. I know that Alice Miller is on the side of the child and that she advocates that they must identify the "sins" of the parent. I know that she believes that the abused child must feel and express complete anger at the parent—that they neither forget what the parent has done to them nor spare them. Yet, as much as her work has moved me, I feel she stops short when she does not adequately address the unmet needs—the unfinished business—of the mother.

How bad do the consequences have to get before we consider the needs of the mother to be as valid as the child's? If it is not appropriate for the child to care whether this happens or not, who is going to care about the mother? From my own experience, I know that the mother is going to have to learn to care about herself. But I know that it would be a lot easier for her to do this if she had the understanding and support of other women—women like herself who know how it feels as a daughter to be "wildly unmothered" yet expected to behave toward their children as though they were fully capable and loving—women who "pour from an empty pitcher." If women like this—like me—do not try to understand why we behaved as we did and why these blatantly "bad mothers" behave as they do, then we have done nothing to change the unremitting cycle of abuse and abandonment.

What about Susan Smith who killed her children? Why do we need to care about her? Surely, she does not deserve our concern. At best we say, "She shouldn't have." But do we seek to know what had been done to see that she *wouldn't* do what she did? When we think about a Susan Smith, we say that it must be stopped—this bad mothering. But how do we stop it before the mother becomes one? And how do we keep ourselves from simply scapegoating the Susan Smiths and not seeing her as one of our own?

Perhaps it is beyond us to even fathom how a woman could do what Susan Smith did. I certainly never even felt the feeling of wanting to kill my children. But when I heard about this woman, I immediately felt for her. I identified with her and wanted to go to her. I wanted to know about her and I wanted her to know herself—for her own sake alone.

When it comes right down to it, I don't believe in the archetypes of Bad Mother and Good Mother. I think that they keep mothers in line—comparing ourselves with each type. We can hate, i.e. fear, the Bad Mother or idealize the Good Mother. In the latter case, we can feel shame, resentment, envy and loneliness that we are not like this paragon of virtue. For some of us, this was the "Brady Bunch" syndrome. Now it might be the "power mom" syndrome.

And, while we're thinking about the Good Mother, let us consider how a mother could possibly be tender and strong and capable *and* have little or no self esteem? Let us wonder how in the world a woman could possibly say, *all at the same time*: "I didn't want you—I don't want myself—nobody ever wanted me—I don't know how to get to myself or out of myself—*and* I will always be there for you and I will do what you need me to do and be how you want me to be and I won't betray you?" Can we give our loving attention to this woman who is so strung out and living a lie? Can we support her in her healing? Can we *leave her alone,* not hound her with blame and accusations as she seeks an authentic life? Can we permit and even support her in leaving the life she is living?

When I went to see *The Hours*, I had to leave the theater during Julianne Moore's portrayal of the mother consumed with emptiness and Absence. I still had not achieved enough distance from the time when I felt that way. After several months I rented the film and, as an exercise in self growth and change, I watched the entire film. I was able to hear Moore's character say: "It was death; I chose life."

What's Going On When The Mother Leaves Her Children?

Since I wrote this section, I have talked with women who feel they can make the changes they want to make within the family. I could not do this; I had to leave. This section is an effort to make that necessity intelligible.

The reason the mother has to leave the mother/child relationship on behalf of *herself*, is basically because no one is going to see to it that she finds her life but herself. This, I believe, is a law of the universe. No one can give us our Self or our life force or the reason for our being; we *have to* find them and claim them for ourselves. They are there for us, but when it comes right down to it, if we're coming from zero, we find them only when they get our total attention. Therefore, the mother may have to do the dirty work of liberating herself and, consequently, her family, if she is to find and know herself.

If and when she is willing to leave, she may have gotten to the point where she has made some changes—has some awareness of herself. For instance, she may now sense a value in herself that is not dependent on being needed. She may realize that others have been dependent on her *being there* and that she is not *there* anymore. She may sense that she has been performing and getting emptier and emptier. She may feel that she cannot fill herself with her good intentions, her generosity, or her sensitivity to others. She cannot divert her Self by being more open to others. She knows that she has committed altruistic suicide. And she knows that she wants herself more than any one or any thing else.

I am describing myself here. I have known other women who have left their children, but to save me, I can't or don't remember hearing them express their deepest, personal reasons for doing so. I only remember them as wonderful women who were thoughtful and conscientious about their lives. None took their freedom lightly. I met them in Boston in a support group for women who were not living with their children at that time. There were about eight of us who met regularly, and we were a diverse group in respect to age and class. It was the best support group I have ever been in.

In my case, I had to go against every rule in the book—risk being judged more harshly than any criminal—having no advocate but myself. I knew I was miserable to the point of and including suicide. I was trying to measure up and I was utterly lonely and confused. When I broke, I had only my truth. I knew there was no middle way—it was change or die. I could neither change in the midst of the family nor try any harder.

This is terrifying and it's doable. I didn't think it took courage, for I was saving my life. As I look back though, I realize that I did something quite remarkable. I did what I had to do *for myself*. I had to face the unknown with no assurance. I had to be intelligible to *myself*—to come up with my own understanding and description of what I was doing, rather than buying the interpretation that others had of me and what I was doing. I was removing myself from a dysfunctional family and causing them to deal with stuff that families often deal with only when the mother dies. (Actually, I used to feel compelled to write a letter to my family that said simply: "Just pretend I'm dead.") I had to deal with the fear that I was considered crazy or at best, deluded. I knew in my bones that women were "put away" for saying "No" or "I can't."

I had one thing going for me and in this case, I was extremely lucky and privileged. I had an independent income. I also had the support of The Women's Movement which said that a woman has a *right* to her life. I grabbed hold of that right like a birthing baby reaches for its breath. I had never heard it before, and I wanted it desperately.

We are used to children leaving a family in order to discover and have their lives—to individuate. But when a mother does this, we tend to see her through the lens of the movie *Kramer vs. Kramer*. We see her as deluded and selfish (a designation that will stop almost any mother in her tracks). I hated *Kramer vs. Kramer,* for I knew, when I saw it, that I identified with the wife and mother and her seemingly unintelligible need to get to herself. What I needed and what she needed was a consciousness that a motherwoman's needs count *as much as* those of the other members in a family. Just after I left my family, an acquaintance said to me: "You've taken the sunshine out of their lives." And I had attempted suicide just months before!

When I left, I did not leave "for the children's sake" or so that I could learn to be a better mother. There is a complete adequacy and appropriateness for a mother to get to her life *for her own sake*. This is so hard to justify that saying it is difficult, but we do have a right to our life if we can believe it. I believed it only because I had absorbed the words of Radical Feminism. Only from them did I feel that I had a right to myself and that I needed what anyone needs to have a life. As T. Grace Atkinson says in her bold and flat-out way: "If women were free, free to grow as people, free to be self-creative, free to go where they like, free to be where they like, free to choose their lives, there would be no such institutions as marriage and family." These words are obviously not true for all women—some know these freedoms. But for those of us who don't know them, can we bear to take them to heart and claim our Selves against all the odds?

Mothers And Daughters

Here I consider the mother/daughter relationship only from the mother's perspective. Recently there was a letter in *Ms.* in which a mother noted that her daughter felt that any success on her (the mother's) part threatened the daughter's desire for prominence. I'm sick of hearing about the daughter's need to surpass her mother. What does that mean to the mother whose self esteem may be developing too—who came to this relationship with a weak ego— no sense of herself at all? I'm also really tired of hearing that any discord between a mother and daughter is "natural" or is "just the way that *it* is." Mothers and daughters are human beings and our relationship can be worked with as any other one can—if we both want it to work. I also abhor the desire that some daughters have, which is to be able to tell their mother off without it affecting her. Metaphorically speaking, this says: "I want to kill you without your dying."

Virginia Woolf describes her mother, Julia Stephen, as the "Angel in the House," a persona created, named, described and encouraged by Freud. The Angel was: "intensely sympathetic. She was immensely charming. She was utterly unselfish . . . she sacrificed herself daily . . . she was pure." However, Woolf experienced the dark side of this persona of her mother's. She knew that her mother was not life enhancing and that she stunted her daughter's symbolic growth. And she wants to kill her, in what she feels is self defense. "Had I not killed her she would have killed me." (Quotes are from Woolf's *Professions for Women,* p. 59.)

I can understand this desire for revenge, but I do not like it or approve of it. It does no good in the long run. And anyway, I'm on the mother's side—asking for a new consciousness in respect to how she is seen and treated.

Do daughters think their mothers are impervious? That we have some magic shield called "love"? And then there's the feeling on the part of a daughter that she has a perfect right to strongly tell her mother off and then later to expect her mother to be there when she (the daughter) is "ready" or needs her. Again, I believe that most mothers and daughters are *just* people, and that there's not a perfect one on either side of the relationship. Most of us are growing and changing, if we're lucky. Usually, neither one of us is "finished." We probably do need a lot of space from each other, however, so that we can go through our changes. And finally, there's "matriphobia"—the fear of the daughter that she is or will be like her mother. What she fears is a trait or traits that the mother may not even be aware of and therefore can't control or may secretly fear herself. What needs to happen is consciousness raising on both sides—the mother needs to discover and know her true self and the daughter needs to consider that whatever behavior she fears is one the mother acquired without asking for it. They both "caught" it without asking for it and for the same reason. It's the cause of the "problem" that they both need to consider and address.

These are some of my pet peeves about the mother/daughter relationship and let me tell you that all of the above has been true of my relationship with my daughter.

But now I want to tell you more about that relationship. It

started with her birth. I was awake and thoroughly conscious when the doctor held the baby up, cord intact. I had asked: "What is it?" And he had said: "You tell me." When I realized that "it" wasn't there, I said "It's a Girl!" I was unbelievably grateful and elated. At the time, I had no awareness of feminism. Yet I knew somehow that this girl child was special for me. As she grew up, I willingly acquiesced to and supported her independent and strong spirit. I let her be who she was determined to be. Now I know that I was vicariously identifying with her.

As the years have gone on, our relationship has been a strenuous one—difficult for us both. For one thing, she witnessed my coming into my own. She was fourteen when I left the family and the day I left her, we both sobbed. Neither of us could understand nor cope with what was happening. In our first telephone conversation after I got to Boston, she said: "I don't want you to suffer." I responded: "I prefer to say that I am struggling." Even now, I don't know if she understands that difference for me or that I am willing and able to take it on. What I do know is that when she reached forty one, the age I was when I left, she did know what "True Self" means and her feminist consciousness was equal to mine. This has always been salutary for me—plus knowing that she came to her "knowings" on her own.

I believe that the deepest and most difficult thing we have had to deal with is our symbiosis. In the family, we had been the only girls. Later, as she wanted and claimed her separateness from me, I had to experience how bereft I felt. Even though I had written my Master's thesis on "The Concept and Experience of Separateness" (gleaned from my time away from the family), I was not prepared to lose the understanding and support of the one person who had ever loved me. Of course, she was only doing her thing but I had yet to learn the deepest truth of what separateness means.

Again, I did the work I had to do with my Self. And it is paying off. I can now hold my own with her without being obsessed with losing her. And as I get stronger, she may be able to let go of her sense of duty and responsibility. Not oddly enough, it is feminism— the respect we have for ourselves as women and our honoring of other women's experiences—which connects and helps us.

So this is the real life story of a mother and daughter. What follows is a theory about the mother/daughter relationship based on the story of Demeter and Persephone.

This story is based on a myth that goes something like this: Demeter was Persephone's mother and everything was fine with them until Persephone was abducted into the Underworld by its God/Head. Demeter almost lost it over this loss of her daughter, but as the story goes, she had enough power to bargain with the abductor and get her daughter back for half of the year. Historically, this was about seasonal change—when Persephone was down, there was fall and winter; when she was up, there was spring and summer.

Some feminists have taken the story as a metaphor for the mother's impotence to save her daughter from the rapes of patriarchy, and the daughter's impotence to control her destiny. As such it doesn't do much for me. I do like the suggestion that Demeter was a good mother because she so mourned the loss of her daughter that she moved heaven and earth, so to speak, to get her back (at least some of the time). But, ultimately, I was left with the seeming reality of women's impotence in the face of patriarchy. What could I do about that? Well, luckily, I was helped by another story—one that introduced the influence of Hecate, the wise crone and goddess of the underworld. This is a story that didn't figure into the famous Elusian myth, but which came from a folk story—one passed among the common people. In it, Hecate meets Persephone in the Underworld and serves as a guide to lead her out. She also appears to the disconsolate Demeter and shakes her loose from her grief by making her laugh.

That story worked for me. I like the concept of Wisdom (Hecate, the Wise Old Crone) intercepting the experience of both the mother and the daughter. It is an alternative to the patriarchal rendition of each one's destiny and role. It gives us another story to the one that talks about mother/daughter paradise (which, as daughters, we often don't experience and which as a mother, I *couldn't* experience), defined and overwhelmed by the power of the male/patriarchy. It also changes the story of mothers pissing and moaning when they don't do it right and daughters pissing and moaning because they feel helpless and betrayed by their mother's impotence.

The ways that young women/the daughters "go down" are painfully and unremittingly familiar to us—depression, sexual naiveté, teen pregnancy, eating disorders, addictions, etc. What we are not so aware of ,or concerned about, are the bewilderment, bereftness and emptiness of their mothers. Both women need Hecate's help and wisdom. For the daughter, these could come through a feminist therapist or feminist books such as *Reviving Ophelia, Saving the Selves of Adolescent Girls* and *Ophelia speaks, Adolescent Girls Write about Their Search for Self*. The mother needs to read any feminist book that helps her develop *her* self esteem and the discovery of her True Self's purpose.

What is important, I think, is that the mother and the daughter stay out of each other's way while they are figuring out their separate Selves. The older daughter has got to give up the notion that she knows her mother better than her mother knows herself. The mother has got to keep on keeping on with her search for her True Self, take her eyes off her daughter and not compare.

They have very separate jobs, but the bottom line is that each woman is discovering her Essential Self.

Mothers and Sons

Blessedly, I can write positively about my relationship with my two sons. I like them both. But, of course, there were potential problems. They're men; I'm a woman, and they have both behaved as chauvinists with me. When this first happened, I felt helpless and hurt. But as I have grown and changed, I can challenge them without being afraid of making them angry or of losing them.

The fact that these two men are my sons is absolutely no guarantee that we will have mutually satisfying relationships with each other. Because we both come from dysfunctional families, it is more likely that our connections will be awkward and strained. But I honestly believe that because of all my hard work on myself, it is possible for us to build good relationships with each other. Fortunately, I don't "need" them; I have myself and my work. And as I watch them grow and change, I can be glad for them—not envious of them.

In respect to these men, it is deeply satisfying to witness their coming into their own—to becoming whole human beings. We've talked about their competitiveness and how it's all about being a "real man." Goodness knows I've had to deal with not wanting to be a "real woman", and it all seems to be about the same thing—becoming our True Selves rather than how we're "supposed" to be.

Essentially, it is rewarding beyond measure to be building relationships with these men who I met simply by being their mother.

Mother In The Middle

Finally, I want to talk about an experience that some mothers have which is rarely, if ever, talked about—being in the middle. I do not mean being in the middle of sibling warfare. I am referring to the mother being caught between her mother and her own children – a situation in which she feels that she is the common enemy of each. In addition, she witnesses her mother relating to her grandchildren in a totally different way from the way that she related to her. She sees her mother cherishing her grandchildren, whereas with her she had been withholding and envious. In my case, I didn't acknowledge this reality until many, many years after it happened. It was silenced along with all the other forces operating on us all. It was easier to just stay in denial about it.

When I finally faced it, it became part of the work of claiming myself and my truth. The biggest part of this work was understanding and healing what had happened between me and my mother, plus what was going on between my mother and my children. I had to deal with the fact that my children adored their grandmother and did not want to hear that I had never felt loved or wanted by her. I had to realize that I had colluded in the lie of the happy family that my mother needed to believe. Of course, by the time I faced all this truth, I was also dealing with the pain of always having felt out of the loop—in my birth family and in my marriage family. None of this work was easy and it took a long, long time to do it, but it was so worth it. Because I did it, I have been able to lay it to rest. I cannot change how others saw my mother. And, truthfully, I have only compassion for her, knowing by the way that I know the place from which she was coming. But this has come out of the cauldron of all my self work and the feminism which informs it.

These are some words I wrote in my journal about my mother:

> She didn't know what to do with me—she didn't seem to want to be bothered with me. And she looks so sad in photographs. I don't know if her relationship to me was the reason, or that she married a jealous and needy man or that no one had loved her or that she was talented and smart and gifted and couldn't put all that to work for herself— or that she was brilliant and couldn't recognize it. Or that she was so beautiful and didn't know it or that she was not free. All I know is that I identify with her.

I love these words and I now love the woman they are about. How I wish we could have known each other when she was alive.

Clearly, I believe that it is the mother *role* that is the problem. It is partly that many—most?—women take on this role when they have no other options for their life. It is their feeling that the only "love" they can experience is within this role. If women could know their True Selves and their uniquely personal and true vision, they could make choices about their lives that *fit* them. They wouldn't have to default to a path of least resistance in order to please someone else or because they don't know what else to do or because they were too muddled and lost to themselves and their purpose to know differently. They would do what they were *called* to do. Maybe they would choose to become mothers—and maybe they wouldn't. They would certainly not choose this role as a last resort.

Kathy Newman suggests the following in a brilliant essay, *Re-membering an Interrupted Conversation: The Mother/Virgin Split*: "In order to free the Self from the mother-role, it is essential that we hear back into communicable form the lost conversations that our mothers might have carried on with themselves."

So, as mothers now, we must cultivate our ability to think ourselves beyond this role by developing a conversation with our self and our Self—that is honest. We must continue our interrupted selves—we must stop and think ourselves through. Bless us all.

THE IDEA / MADE
REAL / IS ME
(Some thoughts about thinking)

The title of this piece is a three line poem I wrote.
Again, this is a poetic form using five syllables or less in the first line,
seven syllables or less in the second line and
five syllables or less in the third.

I n the past, when I was told that I thought too much, it sounded like I was doing something wrong. It sounded like a criticism. In response, I felt defensive. I didn't know what the problem was. Recently, after years and years of more thinking, I have decided that this opinion of thinking is clearly not my problem. But I did spend some time wondering why the critics of my thinking "too much" felt that way. Were they (whoever they were) afraid that if I thought—especially about myself and the conditions of my life—I might figure out what was going on? Were they (especially if they were "significant others") afraid that I might decide, while thinking, to change my life in regard to them *and* to me? In other words, were they afraid that as a result of thinking, I might become different—unpredictable and uncontrollable? Whatever their reason, I never stopped thinking and it did change me and my life

Just recently I began to think *about* my thinking. When I decided that thinking is putting words to feelings, I realized that I had started doing that when I was in my thirties and began to write in a journal. Before that I truly had not known how I felt. At first, the words I wrote, in my journal, came haltingly and sparsely—like those of a child. They were mostly words about how unhappy I was. No one, not even I, knew this, for I appeared to be anything but unhappy. I was outgoing and engaged socially. Someone once said that I bubbled like champagne—that I was the friendliest person in town. I appeared to be a good wife and mother. But when I read my first feminist book, *The Feminine Mystique*, I began to sense that I was performing—faking it. I had never realized this, but the more I journaled, the more I came to know that I was a stranger to myself and not at all in control of who I was or would become. It took many, many years for me to know what was going on with me and who I might be. I was thinking myself through and in the process I was coming into being. Hannah Arendt says in *The Life of the Mind:* ". . . [If] you want to think, you must see to it that the two who carry on the dialogue be in good shape, that the partners be *friends*. The partner who comes to life when you are alert and alone is the only one from whom you can never get away, except by ceasing to think." So I began to experience thinking as a dialogue of my Self with my self. When I first started thinking/journaling, I didn't know I had either one.

As I continued thinking about me and talking to me, I asked questions and tried to answer them—honestly. Questions like: What was my insecurity and anxiety about? What was going on when

I felt so threatened by not knowing what to do? Why did I keep doing what was not satisfying, like wanting to be in a relationship or giving parties or getting overly involved as a political activist? And what would satisfaction feel like anyway? I had heard that Pure Love cast out fear. I certainly wanted to not be so afraid, but what would "pure love" *be*? Wouldn't it be a love unmotivated by duty or pity or neediness and if so, how in the world would I get to it? (The poet Hilda Doolittle, known as HD, said: ". . . I go to the things I love with no thought of duty or pity.") What was going on when I tried so hard to make a relationship work and gave myself away? How come I didn't know my value and overvalued others? What was underneath my desperation to know that I had a purpose? A lot of questions, but until I could get answers to them, I was not satisfied. So I kept thinking. And,I got both answers and solutions in the process.

Thinking about these questions and getting clear about what wasn't working filled many, many journals. As I thought about myself, I drew on all the Radical Feminist writing I had read. The lines and passages that I had underlined and reread again and again were ones I returned to again and again. They told me I had a Self worth knowing and a life worth living. When I finally *got* something that had moved me—when I began to practice what these writers preached—it felt like a gift of grace. This took a long time; I wasn't ready until I was ready. I never pushed myself and wrote: "I can't make it come / but I / sure can receive it." *It* is the realization of my true self—my essential self. And I couldn't—wouldn't—have gotten to it had I not thought and thought and thought about it.

Sometimes I have thought of thinking as praying or meditating. These are times when I am feeling lost or lonely or restless or empty and I need that friend who comes alive when I think—when I am alert and alone. When I am not in trouble and am deep in thought, I experience thinking as the articulation of my consciousness. This is the best of times. I'm not seeking—I'm creating—I'm on the growing edge—I go deep into the fertile void.

But however it is for me, thinking is the crucible out of which I come. The idea / made real / is me.

"LIKE AMNESIACS IN A WARD ON FIRE WE MUST FIND WORDS OR BURN"

I have loved this line of poetry by Olga Broumas (her poems, "Artemis" published in *Lesbian Poetry*) ever since I read it because it captures so well the desperation and the urgency of surviving. I know it's not about finding the right word, but sometimes, for me, when I'm writing in my journal, trying to find my self or my way and I'm lost, a word will come to me that is just right. Oddly enough, it's usually just one word and when it happens, I write "tyftw" (thank you for the word) beside the word because I am truly grateful for it. It has freed me up. Now I can move on.

Finding the right word is like praying the right prayer. I am an atheist and I pray a lot. It's praying the right prayer and believing in it that gets me somewhere. If the prayer isn't right I won't really get anywhere. It's like doing the right thing means you don't have to do it again to get it right.

Life seems to be a matter of getting it right. We fumble along, not knowing, and making mistakes, until we change our ways and do the right thing in the right way.

In my life, I was fairly desperate to get it right—wrong action was making me miserable. I had learned bad habits in order to survive and they were hard to correct. But their consequences were what were making me miserable. So I was like those amnesiacs— lost in a haze of not knowing what was going on and not having the words to describe what I needed. It was when the "ward" i.e., the place I was in, "caught on fire"—when I was in danger of perishing, that I realized how desperate I was to survive—to get out—to heal. And it was words that saved me. First, these were the ones I read and then, they were the ones I wrote in my journal. I don't remember which came first—writing in a journal or reading feminist writers. Whichever, they were both about the truth as I experienced it. They liberated me and enabled me to move on.

WHAT FEMINISM MEANS TO ME

I was in my thirties when I first heard about Feminism or "The Women's Movement" as some of us called it then. I don't remember exactly how it came to me, but my first and immediate response was simply: *"I have a right."* After that, everything was different. Everything.

I had an uncanny capacity to find every piece of Feminist writing that was available to me. One would lead to another until finally I had to *do* something about all the consciousness raising that was going on within me. What I ultimately did was leave my marriage family and go to Boston. As I say in the first chapter of this book, I had to get away from all the "noise of the foreground" so I could hear the still, small voice within me. I was desperate to hear it—to get to *know* me and all about me. I became a "woman giving birth to myself." Of course, my family was affected by my leaving—*and I would do it again.* I was dying, and I wanted to live.

So I took myself away and began to walk a lonely, unfamiliar and non-traditional path. It has led me to where I am today—much clearer about and grateful for my life. It has allowed me to grow and change and to believe in what I say in these essays. And I couldn't/wouldn't have walked that path had it not been for the words of Radical Feminist writers.

When I went to Goddard Cambridge Graduate School for Social Change in Boston, I learned that there were several "feminisms"—Radical Feminism, Socialist Feminism and Cultural Feminism were the primary ones. I had been reading Radical Feminist writers already, and they were the ones who touched on every issue in my life—the personal *and* the political. They seemed to leave no stone unturned. They went to the heart of the matter.

For one thing, being a feminist means to me that I am "woman identified." I especially care how women *feel* about their lives and how they come to know some truth about themselves and then make changes in their lives. Feminism means to me that the most important thing that a woman can *do* is to know her true self, and the most important question a woman can ask herself is: "What am I *for*?" The poet Muriel Rukheyser said: "If one woman told the truth of her life, the world would split open." I think of the prostitute, the secretary, the mother, for instance. What if one of these women told *themselves* the truth about how they felt about their lives and then told another woman and then another? This, of course, is what happened in the 1960s and 1970s in Consciousness Raising Groups. I was in two such groups, and they were wonderful. The truth speaking that went on helped us to begin to know our selves better and to identify with other women more. Nelle Morton quotes a woman as saying to the women in her group: "You heard me into speech." This "active listening" was far from "woo-woo" or sentimental; it raised consciousness and it politicized. Out of these groups came the feminist saying that "The personal is political." Women realized that many of their issues were shared with other women and that many of these issues had to do with sexual use and abuse. This was the time when women turned to each other for insight and support in dealing with rape (marital rape, date rape and being raped by an unknown rapist), incest, and domestic violence. The service groups that resulted were primarily run by volunteers and often by women who had been abused themselves. To my mind, agencies concerned with women's sexual abuse have never been the same since this beginning time.

Women's "culture" was also happening at this time. There was an abundance of art and music and theater about and for women. Feminist journals and papers were published. There was a joke: "How many feminists does it take to screw in a light bulb?" Answer: "Three. One to hold the ladder, one to screw in the light bulb and one to write about it." Women's bookstores opened and thrived. It was a wonderful and amazing and gratifying time for those of us who were a part of it. It was called "the second wave" of feminism, the first being the movement of the Suffragists to get the vote for women. It has been stalled by the backlash to its consequences, but it is not over. On my refrigerator is a card that says: "I'll be a post feminist in post patriarchy."

Perhaps now is the time to say that being a feminist does not mean that I am anti-male. Because I am pro-woman does not mean that I am anti-male. I do abhor patriarchy, however. Patriarchy is "*Mani*fest Destiny." It is Colonialism, the kind the government of the United States practiced on the Native Americans. It is Oppression, the kind practiced on African Americans in this country. And it is Sexism—the colonization of women's minds and bodies based on the assumption that men are superior to us and know what is best for us. Patriarchy is global and has been going on forever, it seems.

To counter patriarchy, I do not want to reverse the scene. I don't think I'm superior to men. And I have no desire to turn them into sex objects. I don't want women to become *like* men—substituting the pinstripe suit for the apron and/or settling for irresponsible and unconscious sex. I want women *and* men to dare to be different and to follow the call of their Selves rather than their gender. I don't relish the saying *Viva la difference,* and I would do away with the terms "masculine" and "feminine." A friend of mine pointed out that, when you see a person's astrological birth chart, you don't know whether it's a man's or a woman's. An astrological chart is about personal gifts and challenges and that's what our lives are about—for men and women.

Being a feminist means, for me, that I want neither to be idealized nor demonized. I am offended by being called a "feminazi," and I can't stand being lumped in with the "sacred feminine." "Good men" are doing this now, and I would so much rather they be concerned with raising their consciousness about women's issues than idealizing us as sacred sexual enablers. The thought of a man using sex with a woman (like a temple prostitute) to achieve some kind of desired transformation is abhorrent to me. When men idealize us as embodying the "sacred feminine", it's hard to argue with them—it makes us seem so *bitchy* and can lead to that horrible saying: "What do women *want?*" The question: "What is a woman for?" should only be answered: "For the realization of her own vision." And while I'm talking about a woman being used for someone else's purposes, I want to say that I also hate it when a *woman* says: "What I need is a wife!" Isn't that like an African American saying that what they need is a slave?

These are a few aspects of feminism that I feel passionate about. Another one is the use of non-sexist language. I tense up when I am reading a book that I like, dreading that the author may use the masculine pronoun to refer to someone whose gender is not specific. I could really get into working for a publishing company where my job would be to clean up sexist language in their publications. I would do this by substituting "they, they or their" for "he, him or his"—no hyphenated pronouns like he/she, for they are laborious and unnecessary. I also don't like it when an author substitutes the feminine pronoun for an unmarked referent. Reversing sexism is not my goal.

So why am I a feminist? Because feminism brought me to myself. Nothing else did—no political party or philosophy, no religious system, and not any of my schooling, except my graduate studies at Goddard Cambridge Graduate School for Social Change. There, I was studying feminist thought.

In closing, consider this: when you hear Socrates say: "Know Thyelf," do you see a woman's face? Do you see your own?

SUGGESTED READINGS

Arendt, Hannah. *The Life of the Mind.* New York and London: Harcourt Brace Jovanovich, 1971

Atkinson, Ti-Grace. *Amazon Odyssey.* New York: Links Books, 1974

Broumas, Olga. *Beginning With O.* New Haven and London: Yale University Press, 1977

_____ "Artemis," *Lesbian Poetry, an anthology.* Watertown, Massachusetts: Persephone Press, 1981

Bulkin, Elly & Joan Larkin eds. *Lesbian Poetry, an anthology.* Watertown, Massachusetts: Persephone Press, 1981

Cooper, David. *The Death of the Family.* New York: Vintage Books, 1971

Daly, Mary. *Beyond God the Father.* Boston: Beacon Press, 1973

_____ *Gyn/Ecology, the Metaethics of Radical Feminism.* Boston: Beacon Press, 1978

_____ *Pure Lust.* Boston: Beacon Press, 1984

DeSalvo, Louise. *Virginia Woolf, the Impact of Childhood Sexual Abuse On Her Life and Work*. New York: Ballantine Books, 1989

Friedan, Betty. *The Feminine Mystique*. New York: Dell Publishing Co., Inc, 1962

Friedman, Susan Stanford. *Psyche Reborn: The Emergence of H.D.* Indiana University Press, 1981

Frye, Marilyn. *The Politics of Reality: Essays in Feminist Theory*. Trumansburg, New York: The Crossing Press Feminist Series, 1983

Heilbrun, Carolyn G. *Writing a Woman's Life*. New York: Ballantine Books, 1988

Jeffreys, Sheila. *The Spinster and Her Enemies, Feminism and Sexuality 1880-1930*. London, Boston and Henley: Pandora Press, 1985

MacKinnon, Catherine A. *Feminism Unmodified, Discourses on Life and Law*. Cambridge, Massachusetts, and London, England: Harvard University Press, 1987

_____ "To Quash a Lie." Smith Alumnae Quarterly, Summer 1991

Miller, Alice. *The Drama of the Gifted Child*. New York: Basic Books, Inc., 1981
_____ *For Your Own Good, Hidden cruelty in child-rearing and the roots of violence*. NewYork: Farrar, Straus and Giroux, 1983

Moraga, Cherrie and Gloria Anzaldua, eds. *This Bridge Called My Back, Writings by Radical Women of Color*. Watertown Massachusetts: Persephone Press, 1981

Morgan, Robin, editor. *Sisterhood is Powerful, an anthology of writings from the women's liberation movement*. New York: Vintage Books, 1970

Pagels, Elaine. *The Gnostic Gospels*. New York: Vintage Books, 1989

Raymond, Janice. *A Passion for Friends, Toward a Philosophy of Female Affection*. Boston: Beacon Press, 1986

Rich, Adrienne. *Of Woman Born: Motherhood as Experience and Institution*.

New York: W. W. Norton & Company, 1976

_____ *On Lies, Secrets, and Silence, Selected Prose 1966-1978.* New York: W. W. Norton & Company, 1979

_____ *Dream of a Common Language.* New York: W. W. Norton & Company, 1993

Roberts, Jane. *The Nature of Personal Reality,* (a Seth book). Prentice Hall, 1974

_____ *Psychic Politics: an Aspect Psychology Book.* Prentice Hall, 1976

Spender, Dale. *Women of Ideas (and what men have done to them).* London, Boston, Melbourne and Henley: Ark Paperbacks, 1982

Steinem, Gloria. *Marilyn.* New York: Henry Holt and Company, 1986

Stoltenberg, John. *Refusing To Be A Man, essays on sex and justice.* New York: Meridian, 1990

Woolf, Virginia. *To the Lighthouse.* New York and London: Harcourt Brace Jovanovich, 1927

_____ *A Room of One's Own.* New York and Burlingame: Harcourt, Brace & World, Inc., 1929

www.ingramcontent.com/pod-product-compliance
Lightning Source LLC
Chambersburg PA
CBHW010859090426
42738CB00018B/3446